INSIGHTS

2023

Junko Murao   Akiko Miyama   Tomoko Tsujimoto
Kana Yokoyama   Christopher Cladis

KINSEIDO

Kinseido Publishing Co., Ltd.

3-21 Kanda Jimbo-cho, Chiyoda-ku,

Tokyo 101-0051, Japan

First published 2023 by Kinseido Publishing Co., Ltd.

Cover photo (right)

The city hall of Lowell, MA (© Adrienbisson | Dreamstime.com)

🎧 音声ファイル無料ダウンロード

https://www.kinsei-do.co.jp/download/4173

この教科書で 🎧 DL 00 の表示がある箇所の音声は、上記 URL または QR コードにて
無料でダウンロードできます。自習用音声としてご活用ください。

- ▶ PC からのダウンロードをお勧めします。スマートフォンなどでダウンロードされる場合は、
  ダウンロード前に「解凍アプリ」をインストールしてください。
- ▶ URL は、**検索ボックスではなくアドレスバー (URL 表示覧)** に入力してください。
- ▶ お使いのネットワーク環境によっては、ダウンロードできない場合があります。

◎ CD 00　左記の表示がある箇所の音声は、教室用 CD（Class Audio CD）に収録されています。

このテキストは、IT・ビジネス・文化・環境・技術・社会・科学・ファッション・宗教といった幅広い分野の記事を取り上げています。長引くコロナ禍のもと、国内外でさまざまな変容が起ると同時に、様々なものも生み出されています。このテキストでは、生きた英語を学び、広い視野を養えるよう国内外のさまざまなトピックの記事を選んでおります。また、各章の話題は、ディスカッションのトピックとしてもご利用いただけます。本テキストを授業内でのさまざまな活動にお役立ていただければと思います。

Key Expressions 1
写真の視覚情報を見てトピックへの関心を促す、リーディング・セクション読解のためのキーワードのブランク埋め問題です。キーワードを耳で聞くだけでなく、最初の一文字と語数をヒントにして、辞書も参照しながら解答してみてください。リーディング・セクションの背景知識を構築しながら、辞書を用いて文法も確認する練習問題となっています。

Key Expressions 2
リーディング・セクション中に登場する重要表現や、TOEIC® Tests にも出現頻度の高い語彙を学習するエクササイズです。単なるキーワードの意味理解だけでなく、関連語句や派生語を構成する接頭辞・接尾辞の意味など、単語力増強に必要な情報が盛り込まれています。

Key Expressions 3
話題に関連した構文や語法の練習問題です。基礎的な文法力も試せる問題となっています。

Background Knowledge
リーディング・セクションの背景を構築する短い記事を読み、簡単な速読用の設問を解きます。一語一句訳すのではなく、必要な情報のみを拾い読みするという速読方法（スキャニング）で読んでみてください。語彙の類推力を養うために、問題解答に関係するところには、あえて注は付けておりませんので、辞書を参照せずに解答してみましょう。

Newspaper English
文法確認のセクションです。ただし、網羅的に文法を扱ってはいません。英文記事を読むために最低限必要な文法の基礎知識や表現ルールを学びます。

Reading
本セクションを読むまでに、かなりの背景知識・文法・語彙の構築ができています。ここまでのセクションをしっかり学習しておけば、辞書なしでもほぼ理解できるでしょう。読解の助けになる注は付けていますが、できるだけ注を参照しないで読むよう心がけてください。

Comprehension, Summary
リーディング・セクションの内容が理解できているかどうかのチェックを行います。

Insights into Today's World
リーディング・セクションの記事で取り上げられているトピックに関して、自分の意見を述べる練習をします。与えられている質問をもとに、まずは英語で自分の意見を書いてから、クラスメイトと意見交換をしてみましょう。

以上のようなバラエティに富んだ練習問題を学習することによって、英字新聞やインターネットのニュース記事を抵抗感なく読めるようになるはずです。最後になりましたが、テキスト作成の際にお世話になりました金星堂編集部の皆様に心からお礼を申し上げます。

編著者

　英字新聞を目の前にすると、一体どこからどのように読んでいけばよいのか迷う人もいるでしょう。まずは、以下のジャパンタイムズ紙のフロントページ（第一面）やジャパンニュース紙のオンライン版トップページを見ながら、英字新聞を読む際に知っておくべきことを学びましょう。大きなニュースは繰り返しフロントページで取り上げられることがあります。まずはこのページで、持続性があり、興味を持てる話題を選択し、しばらくそのニュースを追いかけていく読み方がお勧めです。同じ話題のニュースに何度も触れていると、次第に辞書なしで読めるようになるでしょう。

1．紙媒体のフロントページの構成

新聞社のロゴ（Logo）

これは紙媒体のジャパンタイムズ紙のフロントページです。ジャパンタイムズ紙は、ニューヨークタイムズ紙とセットでも販売されており、国内・海外の情報を幅広く提供しています。

重要記事の紹介

各紙面から大きなニュースを取り上げ簡単に紹介しています。

ヘッドライン（Headline）

ヘッドラインの詳しい説明は p.6 参照。

リード（Lead）

記事の書き出しの一段落目のことをリードと呼びます。ニュースの概略が紹介されます。リードには、5Ws1Hの情報ができるだけ盛り込まれます。

キャプション（Caption）

図版や写真に付く説明文のことです。記事を読むときの大切な背景知識を提供しています。先に目を通しておくと記事の理解の助けとなります。

目次

記事のジャンルと掲載ページが提示されます。

2. オンライン版のトップページ

新聞社のロゴ（Logo）

これは読売新聞の英語版ジャパンニューズ紙のトップページです。紙媒体とは異なり、文字数を減らし、視覚情報の多い作りとなっています。ヘッドラインをクリックすると記事全体が読めます。

記事のカテゴリー

各項目をクリックすると、政治・社会・ビジネス・スポーツなど、カテゴリー別に記事を日をさかのぼって読むことができます。

トップニュース
（Top News）

紙媒体でいうフロントページに載る重要記事が紹介されます。

その他の重要記事や特集の紹介

3．ヘッドラインの特徴 ────────────

　ヘッドラインの英文はいくつかのルールに則って書かれています。文字数を少なくし、簡潔に表現するための工夫がなされます。以下にもっともよく使用されるルールを挙げますので参考にしてください。

① 記事を新鮮に見せるために動詞の過去・現在完了が現在形で表されることが多い
　Government renews call for self-isolation「政府再び自粛要請」（*The Japan Times*, April 23, 2020）

② 「進行形・近接未来」や「受動態」では be 動詞が省略され、それぞれ V-ing や V-ed の形で表される
　North Korea facing food shortages「北朝鮮が食糧不足に直面している」
　309 new Covid cases confirmed in Tokyo「東京で 309 名のコロナウイルス感染が新たに確認された」

③ 未来は不定詞（to V）で表されることが多い
　Japanese govt to extend period for subsidies「日本政府、助成金支払い期間を延長する予定」

④ 冠詞や be 動詞は省略されることが多い
　Banks still busy despite pandemic「パンデミックにも関わらず銀行なおも繁忙」
　Fossilized dinosaur egg found in Japan recognized as world's smallest
　「日本で発見された恐竜の卵の化石、世界最小と認められる」（*The Japan Times*, April 5, 2020）

⑤ 情報源を示すためにコロン（:）を用いることがある
　Distancing needed into 2022: study
　「社会的距離の必要 2022 年まで、とある調査」（*The Japan Times*, April 19, 2020）

⑥ 省略や略語が多用される
　tech → technology（技術）　　govt → government（政府）
　uni prof. → university professor（大学教授）
　HK → Hong Kong（香港）　　BOJ → The Bank of Japan（日本銀行）
　VW → Volkswagen （フォルクスワーゲン）

⑦ カンマによって and が省略される
　Earth becomes wilder, cleaner during lockdowns「ロックダウン中、地球はより野性的でクリーンに」

⑧ 短い綴りの語が好まれる
　vie「張り合う、競争する」　　eye「目をつける」　　nix「拒否する、禁止する」
　ink「署名する」　　near「近づく」

4．英字新聞攻略法 ────────────

　さて、新聞全体の構成が分かったところで、どのように英字新聞に親しんでいけばよいのでしょうか。

① 英字新聞の言語的特徴に慣れよう
　英字新聞は、**3．ヘッドラインの特徴**で見たように、ニュースを新鮮に見せるためにヘッドラインを現在形で書くなど、読者を引きつけるさまざまな工夫がなされています。本書では、その工夫に関して **Newspaper English** のセクションで取り上げていますので、問題を解答しながら、まずその特徴を覚えましょう。

② すべての記事を読む必要はない
　すべての記事を隅々まで読むのは大変ですし、その必要もありません。まずは、ヘッドラインや写真などを見て、興味のある記事だけを読んでみましょう。英字新聞に慣れるまでは、できるだけ日本に関する記事を選ぶほうが読みやすいでしょう。

③ リード・写真・キャプションは背景知識を提供するものなので、最初に目を通そう
　記事（特にニュース記事）の本文は、リードに最重要情報が置かれ、パラグラフが進むにつれ情報の重要度が下がってきますから、しばらくはリードだけに挑戦するのもよいでしょう。

④ 特定のテーマに絞って読むようにしよう

　特定のテーマを継続して読む方法が英語学習には最適です。あるテーマに特有の語彙をまとめて学習することができるので、類似テーマの記事なら簡単に読めるようになるからです。

Insights 2023　Table of Contents

Chapter 01

Being Eco-Friendly with Edible Tableware

創意工夫で器もエコに

Ecopresso edible cups (The Yomiuri Shimbun)

Key Expressions 1

🎧 DL 02　◎ CD 1-02

音声を聞いて 1 ～ 3 の（　　）内に適当な語を書き入れましょう。

1. Edible tableware was created as part of a trend which saw people becoming more (e _ _ _ _ _ _ _ _ _ _ _ _ _) conscious.
   人々がより環境に配慮するようになっている流れの中で、食べられる食器が作られた。

2. The cup made of cookie (d _ _ _ _) was named Ecopresso.
   クッキー生地で作られたカップは、エコプレッソと名付けられた。

3. The edible cups have even been used at events organized by (g _ _ _ _ _) brands such as Mercedes-Benz and Armani.
   食べられるカップは、メルセデスベンツやアルマーニなどの世界的ブランドが主催するイベントでも使用されている。

● Key Expressions 2

語彙学習では、対照的な意味の語（反義語）もセットで覚えておくと、効率的に語彙を増やすことができます。

日本語訳を参考に、1～5の語の反義語を（　　）内に書き入れましょう。

1. reusable［再利用できる］　⇔　(d　　　　　　　　　　) ［使い捨ての］
2. generalist［万能家］　⇔　(s　　　　　　　　　　) ［専門家］
3. outside［外側（の）］　⇔　(i　　　　　　　　　　) ［内側（の）］
4. producer［生産者］　⇔　(c　　　　　　　　　　) ［消費者］
5. buy［買う］　⇔　(s　　　　　　　　　　) ［売る］

● Key Expressions 3

日本語訳を参考に、1～4の下線部のイディオムの意味になるように（　　）内に当てはまる前置詞を書き入れましょう。

1. One day, the cafe took part (　　　　　　　) an environment-themed event.
   ある日、そのカフェは環境をテーマにしたイベントに参加した。

2. Then the owner hit (　　　　　　　) the idea of pouring espresso into a cookie cup.
   それからその経営者は、エスプレッソをクッキーのカップに注ぐというアイデアを思いついた。

3. The cups were named Ecopresso and went (　　　　　　　) sale in 2016.
   そのカップはエコプレッソと名付けられ、2016年に発売された。

4. The company set (　　　　　　　) a fitting environment for food production.
   その企業は、食品製造に適した環境を整えた。

Background Knowledge

CD 1-03

木村アルミ箔株式会社について、英文に<u>述べられていないもの</u>を 1 ～ 4 から選びましょう。

　　Kimura Alumi Foil Co. manufactures small cups for separating food in bento boxes. Some of the company's bestselling products in recent years have been edible cups made of *nori* (dried seaweed), *oboro-kombu* (thinly shaven dried kelp) and soy beans.

　　The company used to make cups made of aluminum foil. But as microwaves and convenience stores became more and more common, aluminum liners could no longer be used for bento boxes sold at convenience stores as they are often heated in a microwave. In the meantime, society was becoming increasingly eco-friendly, which led Mr. Kimura to think, "Wouldn't it be great if the cups were edible and wouldn't become a waste?" The first food the company used to make edible cups was *nori*.

The Japan News

Note　aluminum liner「アルミライナー、アルミ製の容器」

1. 弁当箱の食べ物を分けるための小さなカップを製造している。
2. 近年は、海苔やおぼろ昆布、大豆などを使った食べられるカップがベストセラーになっている。
3. コンビニエンスストアで販売される弁当は電子レンジで加熱されることが多いため、アルミ製の容器が使えなくなった。
4. 食べられるカップの材料として最初に採用したのは、大豆だった。

Newspaper English

英文記事では、会社名がよく登場します。英語表記の場合には、末尾に「会社」を意味する単語が正式名称ではなく略称で付くことが多く、その種類は様々です。同じ英語圏でも Ltd. は主にイギリスで使われ、Inc. は主にアメリカやカナダで使われるなど国による違いもあります。

以下の 1 ～ 4 は「会社」を意味する単語の略称です。正式名称のつづりに直して（　　）内に書き入れましょう。

1. Co.　　　　　　（　　　　　　　　　）
2. Ltd.　　　　　　（　　　　　　　　　）
3. Corp.　　　　　（　　　　　　　　　）
4. Inc.　　　　　　（　　　　　　　　　）

Reading

 CD 1-04

Reduce waste with edible tableware

While disposable tableware is everywhere around us — chopsticks, spoons, straws, cups, plates and so on — edible tableware pieces have been growing in number of late. Amid this eco-friendly trend, several manufacturers of
5 these products explained why they decided to produce them.

RJ Cafe in Osaka serves edible cups in two types: one made of cookie dough and the other gluten-free. It was in 2012 that Machiko Hayashi and her husband started the
10 espresso-specialist cafe, which is operated by 10sense Co. — a company where Hayashi is the president.

One day, the cafe took part in an environment-themed event, at which reusable tableware was used. But Hayashi became concerned because the organizers were using a lot
15 of water and detergent to clean the tableware.

Then she hit on the idea of pouring espresso into a cookie cup — the reverse of the popular way of eating sweets with espresso, which is dipping them into the beverage. She used pudding molds to create cups made of
20 cookie dough, coating the inside with sugar to make it more durable. The cups were named Ecopresso and went on sale in 2016. They became popular after customers began posting photos of them on social media.

In 2011, Marushige Seika, a company in Aichi
25 Prefecture, started selling e-trays, edible trays made with potato starch and other ingredients. According to Katsuhiko Sakakibara, the company's managing director, he saw a huge number of disposable trays discarded at a gourmet event he attended more than 10 years ago. That's
30 when he came up with the idea of e-trays. The company gave the edible trays various flavors so people can be eco-friendly while enjoying a nice variety of options. The e-trays come in flavors such as shrimp cracker, onion, sweet potato and grilled corn.

35 Another company that has taken the eco-friendly, edible route is Bourbon Corp. in Niigata Prefecture. It developed

---

of late「最近」

amid...「～の中で」

manufacturer「メーカー、製造業者」

operate...「～を経営する」

president「代表取締役、社長」

detergent「洗剤」

pour...「～を注ぐ」

reverse「逆」

dip...「～を（さっと）浸す」

beverage「飲み物」

mold「型」

durable「耐久性のある」

prefecture「県」

potato starch「片栗粉」

ingredient「材料」

discard...「～を捨てる」

gourmet「グルメ、食通」

come up with...「～を思いつく」

flavor「味」

come in...「～で提供される」

grill...「～を焼く」

a tubular topping cookie called "Corone Cookie," which can also be used as a straw. The edible straw was launched for business use last year. Currently, the company is considering commercializing the product for consumers.

40 It would be nice in an everyday setting to be able to enjoy your meals with some of these items and not have to worry about garbage and cleaning up.

The Japan News

tubular 「筒状の」	
launch... 「～を発売する」	
commercialize... 「～を商品化する」	
garbage 「ごみ」	

Comprehension

本文の内容に合うように、1～3の質問の答えとして適当なものを、a～dから選びましょう。

1. Why was Machiko Hayashi inspired to create her Ecopresso cups?

   a. She was troubled by the excessive use of water and soap when cleaning reusable tableware.

   b. She came up with the idea after attending a gourmet event where edible tableware was used.

   c. She wanted to reverse the usual way of eating sweets with espresso.

   d. She hoped to increase the popularity of her cafe using the power of social media.

2. What are e-trays made from?

   a. Gluten-free cookie dough with a sugar coating

   b. Shrimp crackers, onion, and sweet potatoes

   c. A variety of ingredients, including potato starch

   d. Recycled disposable trays

3. Which of the following is true about the edible products mentioned in the article?

   a. "Corone Cookies" are currently unavailable for purchase by consumers.

   b. Ecopresso cups went on sale in 2012 at RJ Cafe in Osaka.

   c. E-trays come in three flavors.

   d. Bourbon Corp.'s cookie straws are gluten-free.

Summary

DL 03　CD 1-05

以下の空所 1 〜 4 に当てはまる語を選択肢から選び、書き入れましょう。

In recent years, an eco-friendly trend has emerged which involves the design and (1.   ) of edible tableware. Several Japanese (2.   ) have produced unique edible products, including trays, coffee cups, and straws. The creative designers of these items are motivated by a (3.   ) to reduce the wastefulness of disposable tableware, as well as the (4.   ) spent maintaining reusable tableware.

companies　　manufacture　　resources　　desire

Insights into Today's World

DL 04　CD 1-06

以下の対話の空所に、あなたの考えを書いてみましょう。その後、クラスメイトにその内容を伝えてみましょう。

Many companies are striving to make environmentally friendly products. Edible tableware is one example.

What environmentally friendly products would you like to see become more popular?

I hope that _____

_____

In Search of More Fluid Styles of Work

働き方改革でピンチを脱出

Kana Toyono, working at a car dealership (The Yomiuri Shimbun)

Key Expressions 1

DL 05　　CD 1-07

音声を聞いて1〜3の（　　）内に適当な語を書き入れましょう。

1. Kana Toyono (u _ _ _ _ _ _ _) her customer service skills at a Lexus dealership in Funabashi, Chiba Prefecture.

   豊野佳奈氏は、千葉県船橋市のレクサス販売代理店で、顧客サービスのスキルを役立たせている。

2. She (u _ _ _) to work at a passenger service counter for international flights at Narita International Airport.

   彼女は以前、成田国際空港の国際線旅客サービスカウンターで働いていた。

3. Data shows that people are (s _ _ _ _ _ _ _ _) for more fluid styles of work amid the protracted coronavirus pandemic.

   長引くコロナウイルスの世界的流行のさなか、人々はより流動的な働き方を求めているというデータがある。

Key Expressions 2

1 ～ 5 の空所内に適当な前置詞を書き入れ、「役割」「部分」などを意味する part を使った熟語を完成させましょう。また、レクサス船橋と豊野氏相互の立場について説明した下の英文中の空所に当てはまる熟語を 1 ～ 5 の中から選び、必要であれば形を変えて書き入れましょう。

1. (　　　　　) one's part ［〜としては、〜の立場からすると］
2. (　　　　　) a part of ... ［〜の一環として］
3. (　　　　　) the most part ［大部分は］
4. (　　　　　) part ［部分的に、幾分］
5. take part (　　　　　) ... ［〜に加わる］

Lexus Funabashi is aiming to tap into the customer service know-how fostered at airlines. (　　　　　　　　　　　　　), Toyono is gaining insight by working at the auto dealer.

Notes　tap into... 「〜を利用する」　foster... 「〜を培う」　gain insight 「見識を深める」

Key Expressions 3

経済に関する記事では数字の増減を表す表現が頻出します。1 ～ 3 の空所に当てはまる語を選択肢から選び、形を変えて書き入れましょう。

1. The number of workers on loan in fiscal 2020 has (　　　　　　　　　　) compared to the previous year.
   2020 年度の出向者数は前年度と比べて急増している。

2. In the midst of the coronavirus pandemic, performance of the tourism industry has (　　　　　　　　　).
   コロナウイルスの世界的大流行のさなか、観光業界の業績が急落している。

3. An (　　　　　　　　　　) number of companies are allowing workers to take on second jobs as wages have (　　　　　　　　　) for many during the pandemic.
   コロナ禍のさなか、多くの人の賃金が減少したことから、社員に副業を認める企業が増えている。

decrease　　increase　　nose-dive　　jump

Background Knowledge

CD 1-08

働き方改革の調査結果について、英文に述べられているものを1〜4から選びましょう。

According to the Industrial Employment Stabilization Center of Japan, which acts as a broker between companies involving workers on loan, the number of such workers totaled 3,061 in fiscal 2020, an about 150% increase from fiscal 2019.

Recruit Co. conducted a poll in the spring and found that roughly 63% of about 1,000 people who had begun searching for new employment said they did so because of the pandemic. With multiple responses allowed, 35% of respondents, the largest share, said they "felt uncertain over the company's strategy and its course of action" amid the pandemic, while 26% said they "wanted to do more fulfilling work."

The Japan News

Notes　Industrial Employment Stabilization Center of Japan「財団法人産業雇用安定センター」 poll「世論調査」 multiple responses「複数回答」

1. 産業雇用安定センターの調査によると、2020年度の出向者数は前年度より1.5倍に増加した。
2. リクルートの調査によると、調査対象者の6割を超える人が、再就職をしようと思ったきっかけは不況だと回答している。
3. リクルートの調査において、およそ3割の回答者が他社の企業戦略に魅力を感じたと答えている。
4. リクルートの調査によると、現在仕事にやりがいを感じている人はほとんどいなかった。

Newspaper English

新聞記事のheadline（見出し）では、しばしば冠詞やbe動詞が省略されます。語数を減らすことで文字を大きく提示し、メッセージのインパクトを強める効果があります。

以下のヘッドラインに省略されている語を補い完全な文の形にし、日本語に訳しましょう。

Japanese employees exploring new work options amid coronavirus pandemic

→ Japanese employees (　　　　　　　　　) exploring new work options amid (　　　　　　　) coronavirus pandemic.

日本語訳：_____

_____

Reading

 CD 1-09

Japanese employees exploring new work options amid coronavirus pandemic

The way employees work has become more diverse and fluid amid the protracted coronavirus pandemic, leading to new work styles as an increasing number of people are on loan, taking second jobs or switching companies 5 entirely.

The travel and restaurant industries, among others, have been especially hard hit, although many workers are choosing to view the predicament positively as an opportunity.

10 "Good morning," Kana Toyono said cheerfully at Lexus Funabashi in Funabashi, Chiba Prefecture, as a customer entered the Toyota Motor Corp. luxury brand dealership. She then led the customer to a meeting room for discussions.

15 Toyono, 35, is employed by a firm affiliated with Japan Airlines group but has been working on loan at the Lexus dealership since February this year, mainly greeting customers and answering the phone.

As the number of airline passengers has nose-dived 20 amid the pandemic, the JAL group had up to about 1,800 employees a day working outside their main workplace, including some on loan, as of Sept. 6.

Toyono has been with the airline for seven years and had been working at a passenger service counter for 25 international flights at Narita International Airport. When asked last December about being loaned to another company, she accepted the offer, hoping it would increase her skills.

Lexus Funabashi is aiming to tap into the customer 30 service know-how fostered at airlines. For her part, Toyono is gaining insight by working at the auto dealer. "Speed is vital at an airline's customer service counter, but a more courteous response is required here," Toyono said. "This is a valuable lesson."

35 An increasing number of companies are also allowing

diverse「多様な」

switch companies「転職する」
entirely「完全に」
among others「なかでも」

view... as ~「…を～とみなす」
predicament「ピンチ、苦境」
cheerfully「朗らかに」

affiliated with...「～の系列の、グループの」

up to...「最大～」

as of...「～の時点で」

courteous「丁寧な」

workers to take on second jobs as wages have decreased for many during the pandemic.

take on... 「～を請け負う、引き受ける」

Since last July, Kirin Holdings Co. has allowed employees to have side jobs to deepen their knowledge and 40 experience outside the beverage maker. About 40 staff have taken up such work, with some making use of their expertise to write articles or give lectures, while others do design work.

beverage 「飲料」

make use of... 「～を利用する」

expertise 「専門知識」

Daiki Kaneda, 27, was in charge of sales to eateries, 45 which are struggling amid the pandemic. In August last year, he began working on the side at a firm managing sports clubs where he was an intern during his college days.

be in charge of... 「～を担当している」

eatery 「飲食店」

struggle 「苦しむ」

work on the side 「副業する」

Kaneda works once or twice a week at night distributing 50 a series of online seminars about the life outlooks of corporate managers and top athletes.

distribute... 「～を配信する」

life outlook 「人生観」

corporate manager 「会社経営者」

"By working at both a large company and a start-up, I can see matters more objectively," Kaneda said.

The Japan News

start-up 「新興企業」

objectively 「客観的に」

Comprehension

本文の内容に合うように、1と2の質問の答えとして適当なものを、3の英文を完成させるのに適当なものを、a～dから選びましょう。

1. Why did Kana Toyono accept the job at the Lexus dealership?

    a. After working for an airline company for seven years, she wanted to find a new job.

    b. She could earn a higher wage working at the new position.

    c. Her job at the airline was too fast-paced and stressful.

    d. She hoped the experience would broaden her set of skills.

2. Which working trend is NOT mentioned as a result of the coronavirus pandemic?

    a. Companies are loaning their employees out to work at other companies.

    b. Start-up companies are more successful than large corporations.

    c. Workers are taking on additional employment to make more money.

    d. A growing percentage of the Japanese workforce are choosing to change companies.

3. Daiki Kaneda

    a. circulates seminars about the life outlooks of a selection of successful people.

    b. stopped working at an eatery to return to the company where he used to intern.

    c. works every night for a second company after his primary job is completed.

    d. is one of 1,800 Kirin Holdings Co. employees who are on loan to other companies.

Summary

 DL 06   CD 1-10

以下の空所 1 ～ 4 に当てはまる語を選択肢から選び、書き入れましょう。

> In order to survive and thrive during the (¹·   )
> downturn caused by the (²·   ) coronavirus
> pandemic, a number of Japanese workers are exploring alternative job
> opportunities. While this may mean taking on (³·   )
> kinds of jobs than they are used to, many are viewing it as an opportunity to
> expand their skill set. This trend and the (⁴·   )
> knowledge and insights gained can benefit both workers and companies.

         deep   different   long-lasting   economic

Insights into Today's World

 DL 07   CD 1-11

以下の対話の空所に、あなたの考えを書いてみましょう。その後、クラスメイトにその内容を伝えてみましょう。

> The coronavirus pandemic forces us to think about how we work. For example, more and more companies are allowing their employees to work remotely.
> **Would you prefer to work remotely or go to the office? Why?**

> I would like to _____
>
> _____

Chapter 03

Cats Don't Look, but They Know

見ていないけど知っている

A cat engages in an experiment (Provided by Saho Takagi)

Key Expressions 1

 DL 08　◉ CD 1-12

音声を聞いて 1 ～ 3 の（　　）内に適当な語を書き入れましょう。

1. Cats often show no (r _ _ _ _ _ _ _) to their owner's voice.
   猫は飼い主の声に反応しないことがよくある。

2. This action does not mean the (f _ _ _ _ _ _) dislike their masters.
   この行為は猫が飼い主を嫌いということではない。

3. A study found that the action shows that they are (t _ _ _ _ _ _ _) people with their sense of hearing.
   ある研究によると、その行為は猫が聴覚で人を追跡していることを示していると分かった。

Key Expressions 2

接尾辞 -tive, -ive は動詞の語尾に付き、「〜の性質を持つ、〜の傾向がある」などの意味を表す形容詞になります。動詞の語尾が変化することもあるため、付ける際には注意しましょう。

1 〜 5 の動詞に接尾辞 -tive または -ive を付けて形容詞に書き換え、（　　）内に書き入れましょう。

1. compare［比較する］ → (　　　　　　　　　　　　　) ［比較の、相対的な］
2. cognize［認知する］ → (　　　　　　　　　　　　　) ［認知の、認識による］
3. perceive［知覚する］ → (　　　　　　　　　　　　　) ［知覚の、知覚の鋭い］
4. sense［感じる］ → (　　　　　　　　　　　　　) ［敏感な、神経質な］
5. indicate［示唆する］ → (　　　　　　　　　　　　　) ［示す、暗示する］

Key Expressions 3

日本語訳を参考に、1 〜 3 の英文の（　　　　）内に当てはまる語を選択肢から選び、必要であれば形を変えて書き入れましょう。

1. Cats often (　　　　　　　　　　　　) their faces away when their owners repeatedly call their names.
   猫は飼い主が何度も名前を呼んでも顔をそむけることがよくある。

2. Takagi and the other researchers believed that cats (　　　　　　　　　　　　) on auditory perception to grasp their surroundings.
   高木氏と他の研究者たちは、猫は周辺の環境を把握するのに聴覚に頼るのだと考えた。

3. When the felines became (　　　　　　　　　　　　) to hearing the voice outside the room, they showed no reaction.
   猫たちが部屋の外の声を聞くことに慣れると、反応を示さなくなった。

accustom　　turn　　rely

Background Knowledge CD 1-13

猫の行動を研究している高木佐保氏と彼女の研究について、英文に述べられているものを 1 〜 4 から選びましょう。

Saho Takagi, who is a cat owner, noted that fewer research studies have been done about felines' mental and behavioral mechanisms than those about dogs, although both animals are popular as pets.

"Experiments likely cannot be carried out smoothly since cats do not follow humans' commands," said Takagi, who is affiliated with the Japan Society for the Promotion of Science.

The Asahi Shimbun Asia & Japan Watch

Note Japan Society for the Promotion of Science「日本学術振興会」

1. 研究者の高木氏は、自身の研究のために猫を飼った。
2. 犬よりも猫の方が、心理面と行動面のメカニズムに関する研究報告は多い。
3. ペットとしては今では犬より猫の方が人気である。
4. 猫は人間の命令に従わないので、実験が手間取ることもある。

Newspaper English

ヘッドライン（見出し）は読者の目を引くために文字数を減らし、大きく掲載する必要があります。文字数を減らす工夫として、以下のように情報源（ソース）を表したり、概要を表したりするときにコロン（：）が用いられます。

WHO: Too soon to treat COVID-19 like flu

WHO（世界保健機関）、コロナウイルスをインフルエンザ同様に治療するには早すぎると発表 [*The Reuters*, Jan 13, 2022]

Wanted: Tottori seeks look-alike of nearly 2,000-year-old man

募集中、鳥取県がおよそ 2,000 年前の人のそっくりさんを募集した [*The Japan News*, Feb 12, 2022]

上記の説明を参考に、以下のヘッドラインを日本語に訳し、コロンがどのような役割をしているか考えてみましょう。

Study: Cats know masters' location through hearing, not sight

日本語訳：＿＿＿＿＿＿＿＿＿＿＿＿＿＿＿＿＿＿＿＿＿＿＿＿＿＿＿＿＿＿＿

＿＿＿＿＿＿＿＿＿＿＿＿＿＿＿＿＿＿＿＿＿＿＿＿＿＿＿＿＿＿＿

コロンの役割：＿＿＿＿＿＿＿＿＿＿＿＿＿＿＿＿＿＿＿＿＿＿＿＿＿＿＿＿

Reading

Study: Cats know masters' location through hearing, not sight

Cats apparently pinpoint their masters' locations through auditory signals, not by sight, according to a research team.

pinpoint... 「～の場所が分かる、特定する」

Felines often turn their faces away when their names
5 are repeatedly called by their owners. This action does not mean the cats dislike their masters but instead shows that they are tracking people with their sense of hearing, the researchers from Kyoto University and elsewhere said.

Team member Saho Takagi, a research fellow
10 specializing in comparative cognitive science at Azabu University who previously worked at Kyoto University, wondered how cats cognize the world around them.

comparative cognitive science 「比較認知科学」

wonder... 「～だろうかと思う、疑問に思う」

Takagi and the other researchers believed that cats rely on auditory perception to grasp their surroundings, given
15 that a cat's ear comprises more than 20 kinds of muscle that can move the sensory organs to the right and left separately.

comprise... 「～で成り立つ」
sensory 「感覚の」

To test their hypothesis, they collected 50 cats from willing owners and feline cafe operators. Each cat was
20 placed alone in a room. The prerecorded voice of the master calling out the pet's name was played through a speaker outside the room on five occasions.

willing 「協力的な」
operator 「事業主」

occasion 「回」

When the felines became accustomed to hearing the voice outside the room, they showed no reaction. However,
25 when the same voice was played for the sixth time inside the room, 4 meters from the outdoor speaker, the cats displayed signs of surprise, such as looking around. If a different voice was played on the sixth try, the cats did not act surprised. They also showed hardly any reaction if the
30 sixth sound was made inside the room after electronic sounds or meowing of other cats had been played outside the room several times.

meow 「ニャーと鳴く」

The results, according to the team, suggest cats decide auditorily where their masters are, and they express
35 surprise if their owners' voices come suddenly from a

auditorily 「耳で、聴覚で」

different, impossible location. Other people's voices and other cats' meowing were not enough to surprise them, likely because cats feel it is unnecessary to distinguish those noises.

40 "Felines see their masters in their minds even when owners are out of sight," Takagi said.

Despite the simple design of the experiment, Takagi and other team members faced difficulties in all phases of their endeavor, including securing the needed number of cats,
45 making the felines complete the test, and devising an objective indicator of surprise for a peer review.

The team's findings have been published in the scientific journal *Plos One*.

The Asahi Shimbun Asia & Japan Watch

endeavor「試み」
devise...「～を考案する」
objective「客観的な」

参考
peer review（l. 46）「査読」：論文が研究誌に掲載されるために必要な、研究者仲間や同分野の専門家による審査のこと。

Comprehension

本文の内容に合うように、1と2の英文を完成させるのに適当なものを、3の質問の答えとして適当なものを、a～dから選びましょう。

1. Cats
    a. tend not to have a deep connection with their masters.
    b. have a complex muscular structure in their ears.
    c. do not have the ability to distinguish the face of their owner.
    d. have a sense of sight that is stronger than their sense of hearing.

2. The cats were surprised during the experiment when
    a. they heard the voice of someone who was not their owner.
    b. researchers played a recording of other cats meowing.
    c. they could not find other cats around them.
    d. the voice of their master came from a speaker in the same room.

3. What was one of the challenges the researchers faced when designing their study?

    a. Finding enough cat owners who were willing to record their voices

    b. Choosing the number of times the voice recordings should be played

    c. Deciding on how to identify whether the cats were surprised

    d. Making the design of the experiment less complicated

Summary

 DL 09   CD 1-15

以下の空所 1 〜 4 に当てはまる語を選択肢から選び、書き入れましょう。

> Overcoming several (¹·   ) problems, a team of
> researchers conducted a (²·   ) study of fifty cats.
> The results demonstrated that cats use their (³·   )
> sense of hearing, rather than sight, to perceive the world around them. The cats
> observed indicated an ability to distinguish (⁴·   )
> sounds, specifically the ability to identify the location of their owners.

        challenging   cognitive   important   powerful

Insights into Today's World

 DL 10    CD 1-16

以下の対話の空所に、あなたの知っていること書いてみましょう。その後、クラスメイトにその内容を伝えてみましょう。

I read about this interesting study on cat behavior and finally understood why my cat doesn't show any reaction to my voice. I didn't know they track their masters with their sense of hearing!
Do you know any interesting facts about animals that tend to be kept as pets?

I heard that _____

_____

Challenges of a High School Entrepreneur

逆境をビジネスに

Jiei Kato, CEO of Crystalroad, Inc. (The Mainichi)

● Key Expressions 1

🎧 DL 11   ◉ CD 1-17

音声を聞いて1〜3の（　　）内に適当な語を書き入れましょう。

1. Jiei Kato is introducing a hoodie that is stylish and can be worn comfortably by anyone, (r _ _ _ _ _ _ _ _) of hypersensitivity to touch.

   加藤路瑛さんが、触覚過敏に関わりなく、おしゃれで、誰もが快適に着られるパーカーを紹介している。

2. According to the Ministry of Health, Labor and Welfare website and other sources, hyperesthesia (r _ _ _ _ _) to a state of extreme sensitivity to sight, sound, touch, taste and/or smell.

   厚生労働省のホームページなどのソースによると、感覚過敏症とは、視覚、聴覚、触覚、味覚、嗅覚などに対して五感が極度に敏感な状態をいう。

3. He has (l _ _ _ _ _ _ _) a crowdfunding campaign to produce a line of clothing comfortable for people with hypersensitivity.

   彼は、感覚過敏の人に快適な衣服ブランドを生み出すため、クラウドファンディングのキャンペーンを始めた。

Key Expressions 2

動詞の過去形を作るときに語尾に -ed を付けるのではなく、それ以外の活用をするものを不規則動詞と呼びます。辞書の見出し語は原形で掲載されているため、不規則動詞の変化のパターンを覚えておくと辞書を引く際に役立ちます。

例にならって、1～5の動詞の活用形を（　　）内に書き入れ、意味を選択肢から選び［　　］内に書き入れましょう。

例：think - (thought) - (thought)［考える］

1. wear　- (　　　　　　　　) - (　　　　　　　　)［　　　　　　　　］
2. lend　- (　　　　　　　　) - (　　　　　　　　)［　　　　　　　　］
3. find　- (　　　　　　　　) - (　　　　　　　　)［　　　　　　　　］
4. fall　- (　　　　　　　　) - (　　　　　　　　)［　　　　　　　　］
5. spin　- (　　　　　　　　) - (　　　　　　　　)［　　　　　　　　］

紡ぐ、作り上げる　　　落ちる　　　着る　　　見つける　　　貸す

Key Expressions 3

as には色々な用法があり、文脈によって意味が変化します。as の意味に注意しながら、1～5の下線部の日本語訳を空所に書き入れましょう。

1. As a child, Kato thought that everyone put up with the pain of wearing clothes.

   _____、加藤さんはみんな服を着る痛みを我慢しているのだと思っていた。

2. As part of his work, he set up a laboratory.

   _____、彼は研究所を設立した。

3. He tries to choose undergarments that hurt as little as possible.

   彼は、_____下着を選ぶようにしている。

4. Hyperesthesia limits his food choices as well.

   感覚過敏症は、彼の食べ物の選択肢_____制限している。

5. He wishes he could walk the streets dressed the same way as young people of his generation.

   彼は、同世代の_____街を歩けたらなあと願っている。

Background Knowledge

 CD 1-18

加藤路瑛さんについて、英文に<u>述べられていないもの</u>を 1 ～ 4 から選びましょう。

Jiei Kato launched Crystalroad Inc. in 2018 with his mother Satomi when he was in his first year of middle school. The two began offering support to parents and children seeking to start businesses together, like them, but the business failed to take off. Kato's father, an employee of a company, said, "As part of your work, maybe you should tackle the adverse circumstances you face."

In 2020, Kato founded Kabin Lab, an organization under Crystalroad that distributes information on hyperesthesia and develops products for those with the condition.

The Mainichi

1. 株式会社クリスタルロードを中学一年生のときに立ち上げた。

2. 母親とともに、起業を目指す親子のサポートを始めた。

3. 起業家に向けて、逆境をビジネスチャンスにすべきだというアドバイスを行っている。

4. 感覚過敏症の人々に向けて情報提供や商品開発を行う研究所を設立した。

Newspaper English

 英文記事では、伝えたいニュースの事実と異なった状況を仮定して、当該ニュースを強調して伝えるのにしばしば仮定法が用いられます。

1 と 2 は仮定法の定型表現を含む英文です。(　　) 内に当てはまる表現を選択肢から選び、書き入れましょう。なお、文頭に来る語も小文字で与えられています。

1. (　　　　　　　　　　　　　) you couldn't enjoy a nice meal because the tastes and smells of the food overwhelmed your senses?

もし食べ物の味やにおいがあなたの五感を参らせて、おいしい食事を楽しめなかったらどうだろう。

2. When his clothes touched his skin, he felt (　　　　　　　　　　) he was being poked with a needle.

彼は、服が肌に触れるとまるで針で突かれたように感じた。

as if　　what if

Reading

15-yr-old in Japan turns hardship with hypersensitivity into fashion, support business

hardship「苦難」

TOKYO — What if just the brush of your clothes against your skin was uncomfortable to the point of pain? What if you couldn't enjoy a nice meal because the tastes and smells of the food so overwhelmed your senses? That is the
5 world 15-year-old Jiei Kato has lived in since he was a small child.

brush「軽い接触」

But at the age of 12, the now first-year high school student from the city of Narashino, Chiba Prefecture, near Tokyo, spun his experiences with "hyperesthesia" into a
10 business connecting those with the same condition. Through these efforts, Kato aims to create a society where everyone can realize their full potential.

realize one's full potential「可能性を最大限に発揮する」

"As a child, I thought that everyone put up with the pain of wearing clothes," said Kato, who wears only a
15 sleeveless undershirt and underwear at home the year round. "I try to choose undergarments that hurt as little as possible, and are comfortable to wear," he said.

the year round「一年中」

Hyperesthesia limits Kato's food choices as well. His go-to meal is rice and miso soup, and he eats shabu-shabu, or
20 thinly sliced meat cooked in broth, five times a week. He says he can eat "karaage" fried chicken, depending on the parts used. But all this is not out of some kind of extreme pickiness. Kato said, "Food smells and flavors are unbearable, and I just can't eat things."

go-to「頼りにできる」

thinly「薄く」
broth「だし汁」

pickiness「こだわり」
unbearable「我慢できない」

25 He confided in his school nurse during his first year of junior high, and was told that he may have hyperesthesia. Reflecting on that time, Kato said that when he looked up the condition after returning home, the symptoms matched his situation precisely, and that "all at once,
30 everything fell into place."

confide in...「～に打ち明ける」

reflect on...「～を振り返る」
look up...「～を調べる」
symptom「症状」
precisely「正確に」
fall into place「腑に落ちる」

However, this did not lead to a real solution to his problems. He later dropped out of middle school and founded Kabin Lab. He currently runs the online community with around 480 members, including people
35 with hypersensitivity to sound, taste, smell, and touch, as

well as their families. Kato's job is to facilitate discussion while generating some form of support for their daily lives. Based on his own experience struggling to find garments that meet his needs, the young entrepreneur also planned
40 to create pain-free clothing. While he has a hard time wearing clothes, Kato said, "I wish I could walk the streets dressed in the same way as young people of my generation, rather than wearing the same clothes over and over again to prioritize how they feel on my skin."

45   He said, "My motto is to live without giving up on the present. I'd like to move forward one step at a time, to develop solutions to everyone's concerns and problems. I'd be happy if many people could lend their support."

The Mainichi

facilitate... 「～を円滑に進める」

garment 「服」

entrepreneur 「起業家」

prioritize... 「～を優先する」

concern 「悩み」

● Comprehension

本文の内容に合うように、1 ～ 3 の質問の答えとして適当なものを、a ～ d から選びましょう。

1. Which of the following difficulties caused by hyperesthesia is mentioned in the article?

   a. Sensitivity to screens, including computers, TVs, and smartphones

   b. Trouble distinguishing between tastes of different types of food

   c. Inability to dress in the latest fashions

   d. Headaches caused by an extreme reaction to smells

2. Which of the following is true about Kabin Lab?

   a. Mr. Kato offers information on clothing brands he likes.

   b. Only people who have overcome hyperesthesia are members.

   c. Mr. Kato's school nurse urged him to set up the institution.

   d. Mr. Kato uses the organization to provide support for its members.

3. Which best describes Jiei Kato's attitude toward life?

   a. Frustrated

   b. Hopeful

   c. Pessimistic

   d. Concerned

Summary

DL 12　　CD 1-20

以下の空所 1 ～ 4 に当てはまる語を選択肢から選び、書き入れましょう。

Inspired by his experiences dealing with hyperesthesia, a 15-year old entrepreneur, Jiei Kato, has founded a company with the aim of fostering (1.　　　　　　　　　) among those who suffer from the same condition. An inability to enjoy food or wear clothes comfortably are among the (2.　　　　　　　　　) he has endured over the years. As he and others like him are unable to wear clothing without experiencing (3.　　　　　　　　　), he hopes to produce "pain-free" (4.　　　　　　　　　) that can be worn comfortably.

garments　　community　　hardships　　pain

Insights into Today's World

DL 13　　CD 1-21

以下の対話の空所に、あなたのアイデアを書いてみましょう。その後、クラスメイトにその内容を伝えてみましょう。

Mr. Kato suffers from a state of hypersensitivity to touch, but it's amazing that he could set up his own company to help people facing similar difficulties!
If you were to start something to help people, what would you do?

I want to _____

_____

Chapter 05

The Ties that Bind Hearts

心を結ぶ日本の伝統美

A Mizuhiki piece created by Kyoko Omoda (The Modern Mizuhiki Association)

● Key Expressions 1

🎧 DL 14　◎ CD 1-22

音声を聞いて 1 ～ 3 の（　　）内に適当な語を書き入れましょう。

1. Kyoko Omoda wants people to have the (o _ _ _ _ _ _ _ _ _ _) to come into contact with Japanese culture through "Mizuhiki."
   重田恭子氏は、「水引」を通して人々に日本文化に触れる機会を持ってもらいたいと考えている。

2. Omoda founded the Modern Mizuhiki Association, and she (s _ _ _ _ _) as its representative director.
   重田氏は和モダン水引協会を立ち上げ、その代表理事を務めている。

3. Omoda's association offers (v _ _ _ _ _ _) courses for learning Mizuhiki, from beginner to advanced.
   重田氏の協会は、初級から上級まで、水引を学ぶための様々なコースを提供している。

Key Expressions 2

接尾辞に着目すると、瞬時に品詞の見分けができるようになります。名詞を表す接尾辞には、「～であること、～の状態・動作・性質」の意味を持つ -tion、-ance/-ence、-ness、「～する人、物」の意味を持つ -er/-or などがあります。

日本語訳を参考に、1～5の単語に適当な接尾辞を付けて名詞にしましょう。

1. connect（つなげる）　　　→ [　　　　　　　　　　　　] （つながり）
2. traditional（伝統的な）　　→ [　　　　　　　　　　　　] （伝統）
3. important（重要な）　　　→ [　　　　　　　　　　　　] （重要性）
4. thoughtful（思いやりのある）→ [　　　　　　　　　　　　] （思いやり）
5. direct（指導する、管理する）→ [　　　　　　　　　　　　] （指導者、管理者）

Key Expressions 3

〈find ＋ O ＋ C〉の形を取る表現の中に、find oneself... という表現があります。…の部分に現在分詞や過去分詞を用いると、以下の意味を表します。
・find oneself ~ing「気付くと～している」
・find oneself ~ed「気付くと～な状態にいる」

日本語訳を参考に、1～3の英文の（　　）内に当てはまる語を選択肢から選び、必要であれば形を変えて書き入れましょう。

1. Omoda found herself (　　　　　　　　　　) for a way to connect to her Japanese cultural identity.
   重田氏は、気付くと自身の日本人としての文化的アイデンティティにつながる方法を模索していた。

2. Students found themselves (　　　　　　　　　　) with the colorful ornamental cords.
   学生たちは、気付くと色とりどりの飾り紐に夢中になっていた。

3. We found ourselves constantly (　　　　　　　　　　) about how to promote Mizuhiki effectively.
   私たちは、気付くといつも、どのように水引を効果的に普及させるかについて考えていた。

smite　　think　　search

Background Knowledge ⊙ CD 1-23

水引について学んでいるメグ・ラングレー氏について、英文に<u>述べられていないもの</u>を1～4から選びましょう。

　　Meg Langlais is from Canada, and she is a 22-year-old university student. Her connection to Mizuhiki comes from her Japanese great-grandmother, Margaret Doi. Last Christmas, Langlais received a Mizuhiki kit from her mother. She was also given some tools and parts for Mizuhiki used by her great-grandmother. Her family could not be prouder of her for picking up Mizuhiki to embrace their Japanese ancestry. "Mizuhiki is not well known in Canada, unlike origami. I'd like others to know the meanings behind the knots, such as long, healthy life or friendship," said Langlais. *Kyodo News*

1. ラングレー氏の曽祖母は、日本にルーツを持っている。
2. ラングレー氏は、曽祖母の使っていた水引の道具やパーツを受け継いだ。
3. ラングレー氏の暮らすカナダでは、折り紙と同様に水引もよく知られるようになってきた。
4. ラングレー氏は、水引の結び目に込められた意味を他の人にも知ってもらいたいと思っている。

Newspaper English

 英文記事では、記事の内容に関連する講座や催し物が一緒に紹介されていることもあります。費用や内容など、読者にとって有益な情報が端的に記載されています。

以下はある水引講座の紹介です。英文の情報を読み取り、1～4の下線部に適切な日本語を書き入れましょう。

> ### Mizuhiki Workshop: Intermediate
> This course is for learners who have already completed the beginner level.
> More complicated knots will be taught over 7 lessons.
> **Fee:** 3,500 yen per lesson or a single payment of 24,500 yen
> **Venue:** Online
> **Contact:** The Modern Mizuhiki Association

対象者：1.＿＿＿＿＿＿＿＿＿＿＿＿＿＿＿＿＿＿＿＿＿＿＿＿＿＿＿＿＿＿

学ぶ内容：2.＿＿＿＿＿＿＿＿＿＿＿＿＿＿＿＿＿＿＿＿＿＿＿＿＿＿＿＿

レッスン料：3.＿＿＿＿＿＿＿円（1回ごとの支払いの場合）／24,500円（4.＿＿＿＿＿＿＿の場合）

Reading

"Mizuhiki" Japanese knot-tying giving connection to cultural heritage

For Kyoko Omoda, 52, "Mizuhiki," or the decorative art of knot-tying, is a special way of connecting people to Japanese culture through gift giving, and she hopes to use her experience to help others find their own ties to the
5　past.

"It's a uniquely Japanese tradition of hospitality that not only puts importance on the gift but reflects the sender's thoughtfulness in putting just as much care on how it is wrapped," said Omoda, who started learning the
10　art from a friend 10 years ago when her family moved to Kanazawa, Ishikawa Prefecture.

Having spent part of her younger life in Kenya and Indonesia, Omoda found herself searching for a way to connect to her Japanese cultural identity upon her return.
15　Mizuhiki proved to be one powerful link.

Kanazawa is one of the places where Mizuhiki has flourished. There, she found herself smitten with the colorful ornamental cords mainly based on thin strips of Japanese-style "washi" paper. The strips are twisted to
20　form knots and reveal patterns, each carrying a meaning such as "longevity" or "eternal bond."

In Japan, Mizuhiki is most often seen when tying packages or envelopes with different patterns for events such as weddings or funerals.

25　Mizuhiki is said to date back to the ancient Asuka period from the 6th to 8th century when an envoy from Japan to China during the Sui Dynasty (581-618) returned home with a Sui envoy who brought gifts tied and decorated with red and white hemp strings. Originally a
30　luxury item, Mizuhiki eventually evolved over the years to a product widely used by the general public.

"There's so much history in Mizuhiki," said Omoda, whose passion for, and acquisition of, Mizuhiki skills made her wish for more formal recognition. She recounted,
35　"There was no qualifying examination for Mizuhiki

knot-tying「結び、紐などの結び目を作る技術」
heritage「遺産」
decorative「装飾の」

tie「つながり」

hospitality「おもてなし」
reflect...「～を反映する」

wrap...「～を包装する」

prove...「～であることがわかる、証明される」
flourish「栄える」
strip of "washi" paper「和紙の紙芯、和紙を紐状にしたもの」
twist...「（糸など）をよる」
reveal...「～を示す」
longevity「長寿」
bond「絆」
envelope「封筒」
funeral「葬式」
date back to...「～に遡る」
envoy「使節」
Sui Dynasty「隋王朝」
hemp string「麻紐」
luxury「高級な」
evolve「徐々に発展する」
general public「一般の人」

recount...「～を（詳しく）語る」

students and I felt it would motivate us more if there was." Eventually, in 2019, she set up the Modern Mizuhiki Association, of which she is the representative director. Based in Tokyo, she turned it into a general incorporated
40 association to give more credibility to the certification program for "Mizuhiki taishi," or Mizuhiki ambassadors.

    "We will not only teach but will also play the role of ambassadors to promote and pass on Mizuhiki in and beyond Japan," said Omoda, who is among the six
45 teachers. The student body, both in Japan and abroad, has now grown to around 200.

Kyodo News

general incorporated
association「一般社団法人」
credibility「信頼性」
certification「認定」
ambassador「大使」

Comprehension

本文の内容に合うように、1と2の英文を完成させるのに適当なものを、3の質問の答えとして適当なものを、a～dから選びましょう。

1. Kyoko Omoda

    a. spent a portion of her childhood living abroad.

    b. is particularly fond of the Asuka-era style of Mizuhiki.

    c. believes Mizuhiki should remain a luxury item.

    d. founded the Modern Mizuhiki Association in Kanazawa.

2. The art of Mizuhiki

    a. is often used to commemorate special occasions.

    b. spread to China during the Asuka Era.

    c. is primarily used by Japanese elites.

    d. originated in Kanazawa, Ishikawa Prefecture.

3. Which of the following is true about the Modern Mizuhiki Association?

    a. It is awaiting approval to become a general incorporated association.

    b. The association offers courses that are open to people living in other countries.

    c. Six Mizuhiki ambassadors share the role of representative director.

    d. The organization employs about 200 teachers based in Tokyo.

Summary

🎧 DL 15　◎ CD 1-25

以下の空所 1 ～ 4 に当てはまる語を選択肢から選び、書き入れましょう。

Japanese "Mizuhiki" artist, Kyoko Omoda, was originally drawn to the decorative knot-tying tradition as a way to cultivate her Japanese (1.　　　　　　　). Her (2.　　　　　　　) for the ancient art form stems from its connection to Japanese notions of hospitality, as well as the deeper (3.　　　　　　　) it conveys. Her (4.　　　　　　) of the Modern Mizuhiki Association allows her to share the tradition with the world through certified Mizuhiki ambassadors.

identity　　meaning　　founding　　passion

Insights into Today's World

🎧 DL 16　◎ CD 1-26

以下の対話の空所に、あなたのアイデアを書いてみましょう。その後、クラスメイトにその内容を伝えてみましょう。

Ms. Omoda is working to spread the beauty of "Mizuhiki," the decorative art of knot-tying.
What kind of traditional Japanese crafts would you want to promote to the world?

Personally, _____

_____

Chapter 06

Insect Funerals

小さな命を葬るとき

The "Insect Heaven" graveyard for pet bugs (The Mainichi)

Key Expressions 1

🎧 DL 17　◎ CD 1-27

音声を聞いて 1 〜 3 の（　　）内に適当な語を書き入れましょう。

1. There has been a sudden rise in inquiries to businesses offering funerals for (b _ _ _ _ _ _) pet bugs in Japan.

   愛するペットの昆虫のために葬儀を提供している企業への問い合わせが日本で急増している。

2. Most of the (i _ _ _ _ _ _) brought in are either rhinoceros beetles or stag beetles.

   持ち込まれる昆虫のほとんどがカブトムシかクワガタムシのどちらかである。

3. The pet bugs are (b _ _ _ _ _) in the "Insect Heaven" graveyard in Hyogo Prefecture.

   そのペットの昆虫たちは、兵庫県の「昆虫天国」というお墓に埋葬される。

Key Expressions 2

以下の1〜4の語句は care を使った熟語です。日本語訳を参考に、（　　）内に当てはまる前置詞を選択肢から選び、書き入れましょう。

1. take care (　　　　　　　　) ...　　　　〜の世話をする
2. care (　　　　　　　) ...　　　　〜が好きである
3. treat ... (　　　　　) care　　〜を丁寧に扱う
4. be (　　　　　) the care of ...　〜の世話になって

under　　of　　for　　with

Key Expressions 3

日本語訳を参考に、1〜4の英文の（　　）内に当てはまる語を選び、必要であれば適当な形に変えて書き入れましょう。

1. The family was reluctant (　　　　　　　　　　　　) the insect away with the biodegradable garbage when it died.

   その家族は、昆虫が息を引き取ったときに生ゴミと一緒に捨てるのをためらった。

2. They were concerned that the bacteria (　　　　　　　　　　) the corpse would affect the local ecosystem.

   彼らは亡骸を分解するバクテリアが、地元の生態系に悪い影響を及ぼすのではないかと心配していた。

3. The father even pondered (　　　　　　　　　) of the insect as combustible waste.

   父親は、その昆虫を可燃ごみとして処分しようとも考えた。

4. His daughter seemed (　　　　　　　　　　) because the company treated the remains with such care.

   その会社は亡骸を非常に丁寧に扱ってくれたので、彼の娘も安心したようだった。

dispose　　relieve　　throw　　decompose

Background Knowledge CD 1-28

株式会社アビーコムの提供するペットの葬儀について、英文に述べられているものを
1〜4から選びましょう。

Abircome Co., which runs Ai Pet Group, launched pet funeral services in 2003. To distinguish itself from other companies, about four years ago, it began services for animals other than cats and dogs, including hamsters, parrots and rabbits. The company launched insect funerals along the same lines and as an educational service. Most adult rhinoceros and stag beetles are bought in early summer and die in autumn. By encouraging children to commemorate the bugs' deaths properly, the company hopes to nurture attitudes that value life.

Abircome director Shinobu Nakata, 48, commented, "The bug funerals have elicited a reaction beyond our expectations. The children are treating their pet insects with great care."

The Mainichi

Note elicit...「〜を引き出す」

1. 競合他社との差別化を図るため、2003 年に犬猫以外の動物の葬儀サービスを始めた。
2. 昆虫葬を始めたのは教育サービスとしてであった。
3. 成虫のカブトムシやクワガタムシが息を引き取るのは夏の初めである。
4. 子どもたちはペットとして昆虫を飼うことを躊躇している。

Newspaper English

 英文記事の中には、関連する写真と写真の説明文（キャプション）が付いているものもあり、記事の内容理解を助けてくれます。誰が、どこで、いつ、何をしているのか、などの情報が盛り込まれる場合があります。

1〜3の（　　）内に当てはまる語句を a 〜 c から選び、写真のキャプションを完成させましょう。また、この人物が何をしているところなのか考えてみましょう。

Abircome Co. director Shinobu Nakata holds a kit for mailing dead insect remains, at 1.(　　　) in 2.(　　　) on 3.(　　　).

a. Sept. 29, 2021
b. Amagasaki, Hyogo Prefecture
c. Ai Pet Ceremony Amagasaki

この人物がしていること：
_____

Reading

Funeral services to honor pet insects gain quiet popularity in Japan

AMAGASAKI, Hyogo — There has been a sudden rise in inquiries to businesses offering funerals for beloved pet bugs in Japan, suggesting a spike in the memorial services' popularity. The Mainichi Shimbun delved deeper
5 into the subject to find out what is behind this quiet trend.

"We got a Japanese rhinoceros beetle as part of my daughter's education, so we were reluctant to throw it away with the biodegradable garbage when it died," said Takayuki Fukui, a 45-year-old father in the city of
10 Nishinomiya, Hyogo Prefecture. His daughter, a primary school second grader, cared for the beetle for about three months before it died in September. They thought of burying the beetle outdoors in a park, but the family was concerned that the bacteria decomposing the corpse would
15 be bad for the local ecosystem.

As Fukui was pondering disposing of the insect as combustible waste, he learned about bug funerals online and decided to apply. "My daughter was feeling sad over the rhinoceros beetle's death, but they (the company)
20 treated the remains with care, so she seemed relieved," he said.

Ai Pet Group, which is operated by Abircome Co., has been offering insect funeral services since 2019. The company has seen its client numbers increase steadily
25 each year. Although it only had around 10 inquiries in 2019, that number increased to about 40 in 2020, and to as many as 100 by the end of October 2021. Most of the insects brought in are either rhinoceros beetles or stag beetles that had been under the care of children of
30 primary school age.

To get a funeral for a dearly departed six-legged friend, people bring in the remains or mail them inside a special kit equipped with a drying agent and cushioning material. The insect is then buried in the "Insect Heaven" graveyard
35 in the Hyogo Prefecture city of Amagasaki, where a

spike「急上昇」
delve into...「〜を掘り下げる、探求する」

drying agent「乾燥剤」
cushioning material「緩衝材」

044

Buddhist priest holds memorial services once a month. The remains are not cremated because the carapace cannot survive the fire. Some bugs brought in even had messages attached, including, "Thanks for coming to our
40 home in such a tiny body," and "Please go to heaven. We won't ever forget you."

cremate... 「〜を火葬する」

carapace 「甲殻」

Abircome director Shinobu Nakata said one reason for the growth in insect funerals is the rising number of people living in urban apartment buildings. He said, "I
45 suppose there are more people who don't have dogs or cats, but instead have small animals and reptiles, as well as insects. The parents who apply for the services also wish to teach the value of life to their children. If they experience memorial services now, it may encourage them
50 to cherish other pets they might keep in the future."

reptile 「爬虫類」

cherish... 「〜を大切にする」

The Mainichi

Comprehension

本文の内容に合うように、1と3の質問の答えとして適当なものを、2の英文を完成させるのに適当なものを、a〜dから選びましょう。

1. Why did Takayuki Fukui's family abandon their initial plan of burying their pet beetle in a park?

   a. Their concern for the local environment

   b. Fukui's daughter convinced him to apply for a bug funeral.

   c. Because of the damage it could cause to the biodegradable garbage

   d. The city of Nishinomiya forbids pet burials in public parks.

2. The services provided by Ai Pet Group include

   a. treatment with a drying agent before cremation of the remains.

   b. message cards in the burial kit.

   c. memorial services of various religious traditions.

   d. burial in a location designated for the remains of insects.

3. Which is NOT one of the reasons that Shinobu Nakata offers to explain the growth in insect funerals?

   a. People choosing to own smaller pets rather than larger animals

   b. The recent simplification of the application process

   c. The rising number of people living in urban apartment buildings

   d. Parents' desire to turn a pet's death into a learning experience for children

Summary
 DL 18   CD 1-30

以下の空所 1 ～ 4 に当てはまる語を選択肢から選び、書き入れましょう。

>   Recent years have seen a (¹·   ) increase in the popularity of memorial services for pet insects. Services provided by companies include (²·   ) handling and burial of the remains, as well as ceremonial rituals performed by Buddhist priests. While one purpose of such services is to dispose of the insects' remains in a responsible way, they also serve as an (³·   ) tool for children, teaching them to value life when they lose their (⁴·   ) pet.

      treasured   educational   delicate   steady

Insights into Today's World
 DL 19    CD 1-31

以下の対話の空所に、あなたの考えを書いてみましょう。その後、クラスメイトにその内容を伝えてみましょう。

The insect funeral services described in this article are great. Our pet parrot, Taro, is young and we can't imagine that his life will end someday, but it's nice to know that this kind of service is available.
Have you ever had to deal with the loss of a pet?

I know how you feel. _____

_____

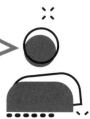

Chapter 07

The History of QR Codes

QR コードの開発秘話

Masahiro Hara, who developed the QR code (Courtesy of Denso Wave Inc.)

Key Expressions 1

🎧 DL 20　　◎ CD 1-32

音声を聞いて 1 ～ 3 の（　　）内に適当な語を書き入れましょう。

1. The QR codes we see all around us were (i _ _ _ _ _ _ _) by a Japanese engineer.
   私たちが至るところで目にする QR コードは、日本人のエンジニアによって発明された。

2. "QR" (s _ _ _ _ _) for "quick response."
   「QR」は、「quick response（素早い反応）」の略である。

3. The (e _ _ _ _ _ _ _ _) of the cell phone is what jump-started the spread of QR codes.
   携帯電話の進化が、QR コードの普及を活性化した。

Key Expressions 2

日本語訳を参考に、形容詞は名詞、名詞は形容詞の形にして空所に適当な語を書き入れましょう。

	形容詞	名詞
1	dimensional（次元の）	＿＿＿＿＿＿＿＿＿＿＿＿（次元）
2	＿＿＿＿＿＿＿＿＿＿＿＿（至るところにある）	ubiquity（偏在、至るところにあること）
3	＿＿＿＿＿＿＿＿＿＿＿＿（季節の）	season（季節）
4	industrial（産業の）	＿＿＿＿＿＿＿＿＿＿＿＿（産業）
5	＿＿＿＿＿＿＿＿＿＿＿＿（効率的な）	efficiency（効率）
6	accurate（正確な）	＿＿＿＿＿＿＿＿＿＿＿＿（正確さ）

Key Expressions 3

付帯状況を表す〈with ＋ A ＋ B〉の形式は、A に名詞、B に名詞の状態を表す語句となり、「A が B の状態で」「A が B をしながら」といった意味を表します。

例：The girl talked to me with her mouth full.　その少女は（食べ物で）口を一杯にして私に話し
　　　　　　　　　　　　　A　　B　　　　　　かけた。

1 〜 3 の英文の［　　］内の語句を正しい語順に並べ替えましょう。

1. A man was holding a box and checking the barcodes [in / a scanner / with / his hand].

   ある男性は手にスキャナーを持って箱を抱え、そのバーコードをチェックしていた。

   ＿＿

2. Barcodes are considered one-dimensional [side by side / with / set / vertical lines].

   バーコードは縦線が横並びで配置されており、一次元と見なされる。

   ＿＿

3. Once the QR code is scanned into the computer, you'll see a pop-up window appear [listed / the QR code's content / in the middle of it / with].

   その QR コードがコンピュータに取り込まれると、真ん中にその QR コードの内容が記載されたポップアップ・ウィンドウが現れる。

   ＿＿

Background Knowledge

CD 1-33

QR コードの使用が広まった経緯について、英文に<u>述べられていないもの</u>を 1 〜 4 から選びましょう。

In 2002, Sharp Corp. introduced a cell phone with a QR code reader to the public. Other manufacturers followed suit. With consumers in possession of scanners, corporations began using QR codes embedded with information linking users to their websites. QR codes spread like wildfire.

With the coming of the smartphone, the uses of QR codes far exceeded Hara and his colleagues' expectations. What surprised Hara most was that QR codes are now used for payments. The online payment platform Alipay, which is under the umbrella of the Chinese e-commerce giant Alibaba Group, began using QR codes to exchange users' payment amounts and other related information.

The Mainichi

Notes in possession of...「〜を持って」 embedded with...「〜が埋め込まれた」 spread like wildfire「またたく間に広がる」 expectation「期待」 under the umbrella of...「〜傘下の」

1. 携帯電話に QR コード・リーダーを搭載したのはシャープ株式会社が最初だった。

2. 多くの企業が自社サイトの情報を伝えるために QR コードを使い始めたことで、QR コードの広まりに拍車がかかった。

3. QR コード開発者の原氏は、QR コードが支払いにも使われることを予想していた。

4. アリババ・グループのアリペイは、電子決済で QR コードを活用し始めた。

Newspaper English

長い名称や用語は、初出の際に "Light Emitting Diode" (hereinafter referred to as "LED") (「発光ダイオード」以下、LED と呼ぶ) などとし、略称を使用するのが慣例です。hereinafter referred to as はしばしば省略されます。

1 と 2 の英文の下線部の語句の略語を (　　) 内に書き入れましょう。

1. Hara set his sights on <u>two-dimensional</u> (　　　　　　　) codes, whose development had begun in the U.S.
原氏は、アメリカですでに開発が始まっていた 2 次元コードに狙いを定めた。

2. The 13-digit number above the barcode on the back cover of your book is the <u>International Standard Book Number</u> (　　　　　　).
本の裏表紙のバーコードの上にある 13 桁の数字は、国際標準書籍番号である。

Reading

From Japanese auto parts to ubiquity: a look at the history of QR codes

Masahiro Hara, who developed the QR code, is an engineer at Denso Wave Inc., an industrial equipment manufacturer in the Toyota Group.

It was 1992 when Hara, then at Denso Wave parent
5 company Denso Corp.'s barcode research and development department, began developing the QR code. At the time, Denso used barcodes to keep track of auto parts. But barcodes can only convert 20 alphameric characters' worth of information. The more information that needs
10 representing, the more barcodes become necessary, leading to one product needing some 10 barcodes. Workers used readers to scan each product's barcodes every time they shipped them. During busy season, several thousand barcodes required scanning, presenting major efficiency
15 challenges to overcome.

Hara set his sights on two-dimensional (2D) codes, whose development had begun in the U.S. While barcodes are considered one-dimensional (1D) with vertical lines set side by side, 2D codes comprise small cells lined like a
20 mosaic, which allows for a lot of information to be included in a small space. But if other shapes or characters were near the codes, the scanners could not distinguish codes from non-codes and took time to read information correctly.

25 After some trial and error, Hara's QR codes were finally born. If you look closely, you can see smaller black squares in three corners of the square. This is called a position detection pattern, which is unique to QR codes. The idea came to Hara when he looked out the window of a train
30 and saw a building with non-matching windows on its upper floors.

Thanks to the position detection pattern, scanners swiftly recognize a QR code and read the information contained within. In addition to fast and accurate reading,
35 the amount of information embeddable into a code rose

industrial equipment manufacturer 「産業機器メーカー」
parent company 「親会社」

keep track of... 「〜の記録をつける」
convert... 「〜を変換する」
alphameric character 「英数字」
worth of... 「〜に値する」
lead to... 「〜を引き起こす」

present a challenge 「課題を提示する」
efficiency 「効率」
overcome... 「〜を克服する」

comprise... 「〜から成る」
line 「並ぶ」
allow for... 「〜を可能にする」
distinguish... from ~ 「…を〜と区別する」

trial and error 「試行錯誤」
square 「正方形」
position detection pattern 「切り出しシンボル」

non-matching 「適合しない、マッチしない」

swiftly 「すばやく」
contain... 「〜を含む」
embeddable 「埋め込むことのできる」

dramatically to 1,800 kanji characters, the equivalent of an A4-size document.

The QR code made its world debut in 1994. Denso chose not to exercise its patent rights for the QR code. Its aim
40 was for the codes to spread widely and boost profits through sales of scanners and other related machinery.

The Mainichi

equivalent「同等のもの」	
make one's debut「初登場する」	
exercise a patent right「特許権を行使する」	
boost profits「利益を押し上げる」	
machinery「機械（類）」	

Comprehension

本文の内容に合うように、1と3の質問の答えとして適当なものを、2の英文を完成させるのに適当なものを、a ～ d から選びましょう。

1. Why did barcodes create efficiency problems for Denso Corp.?
   a. An excessive number of barcodes were needed for each product.
   b. Individual products required up to 20 barcodes.
   c. Scanners had trouble detecting the codes quickly enough.
   d. Alphameric characters contain a limited amount of information.

2. Masahiro Hara developed the "position detection pattern" in order to
   a. reflect the architectural style of a building he randomly encountered.
   b. make QR codes more recognizable for scanners.
   c. improve the unique appearance of QR codes.
   d. contain the vertical lines of QR codes which are set side by side.

3. Which of the following is NOT an advantage of QR codes?
   a. They make efficient use of the space they occupy.
   b. Their code can contain several thousand kanji characters.
   c. Scanners can read them quickly and accurately.
   d. They can store more information than barcodes.

Summary

DL 21　CD 1-35

以下の空所 1 ～ 4 に当てはまる語を選択肢から選び、書き入れましょう。

Masahiro Hara, the Japanese engineer who invented QR codes, (1.　　　　　　　　) developed the mosaic-like codes with the aim of creating a method of (2.　　　　　　　　) tracking auto parts. The two-dimensional nature of QR codes (3.　　　　　　　　) increased the amount of information that could be contained in a limited space. Additionally, the unique design allows for quick detection of the (4.　　　　　　　　) used codes.

vastly　　widely　　efficiently　　originally

Insights into Today's World

DL 22　CD 1-36

以下の対話の空所に、あなたの考えを書いてみましょう。その後、クラスメイトにその内容を伝えてみましょう。

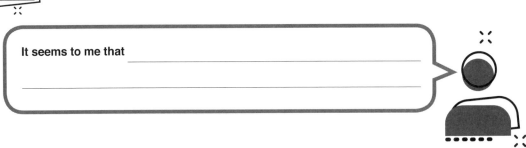

Denso Wave Inc. invented the QR code in 1994 to make manufacturing operations more efficient. Since then, it has come into wide general use. **Which do you think was the most important factor behind its spread?**

It seems to me that _____

_____

Chapter 08

Afghanistan's Bacha Posh

男の子として生きるか、女の子として生きるか

Sanam sits among Afghan boys (AP/Aflo)

Key Expressions 1

🎧 DL 23　◎ CD 1-37

音声を聞いて 1 ～ 3 の（　　）内に適当な語を書き入れましょう。

1. Sanam is (c _ _ _ _ _) a bacha posh: a girl living as a boy.
   サナムは、バチャポッシュ―つまり男の子として生活する女の子―と呼ばれる。

2. She enjoys playing soccer and cricket with boys, wrestles with the
   (n _ _ _ _ _ _ _ _ _ _) butcher's son and can work to help the family make a
   living.
   彼女は少年たちとサッカーやクリケットを楽しみ、近所の肉屋の息子とレスリングをし、家族の家計を
   助けるため働くことができる。

3. Once a bacha posh reaches puberty, she is expected to (r _ _ _ _ _) to traditional
   girls' gender roles.
   バチャポッシュが年頃になると、伝統的な少女のジェンダーの役割に戻ることが望まれる。

Key Expressions 2

1～5は本文に出てくるフレーズです。日本語訳を参考に（　　）内に適当な動詞を選択肢から選び、書き入れましょう。

1. (　　　　　　) boys' clothes　　　　　　［男の子の服を身につける］
2. (　　　　　　) ends meet　　　　　　　　［家計を支える］
3. (　　　　　　) power　　　　　　　　　　［権力を握る］
4. (　　　　　　) women from working　［女性が働くことを禁止する］
5. (　　　　　　) with an issue　　　　　　［問題に対処する］

bar　　deal　　make　　seize　　don

Key Expressions 3

過去のある時点で起こった出来事は基本的に過去時制で述べられますが、常に変わらない事実は現在時制で述べられます。1～3の（　　）内に当てはまる動詞を選択肢から選び、適当な時制にして書き入れましょう。

1. Sanam's father, already suffering from a back injury, (　　　　　　　　　　)
   his job as a plumber.
   サナムの父親はすでに腰を痛めており、配管工としての仕事を失った。

2. He (　　　　　　　　　　) to selling coronavirus masks on the streets,
   making the equivalent of $1-$2 per day. But he (　　　　　　　　　　)
   a helper.
   彼は通りでコロナウイルスのマスクを売るようになり、一日1、2ドル相当を稼いでいたが、手伝ってくれる人が必要だった。

3. The family (　　　　　　　　　　) four daughters and one son, but
   their 11-year-old boy does not have full use of his hands following an injury. So
   the parents said they (　　　　　　　　　　) to make Sanam, their
   daughter, a bacha posh.
   その家族には4人の娘と1人の息子がいるが、11歳の息子はけがをした後両手が十分に使えない。そのため両親は娘のサナムをバチャポッシュにすることに決めたと述べた。

need　　have　　lose　　decide　　turn

Background Knowledge

 CD 1-38

少女が少年として生きる慣習について、英文に<u>述べられていないもの</u>を 1 ～ 4 から選びましょう。

　It is unclear where the practice originated or how old it is, and it is impossible to know how widespread it might be. A somewhat similar tradition exists in Albania, another deeply patriarchal society, although it is limited to adults. Under Albania's "sworn virgin" tradition, a woman would take an oath of celibacy and declare herself a man, after which she could inherit property, work and sit on a village council — all of which would have been out of bounds for a woman.

The Associated Press

Notes patriarchal「家父長制の」 sworn virgin「宣誓処女」 celibacy「貞節」 out of bounds「禁じられて」

1. この慣習の起源は明らかではないが、どのように広まったのかは知られている。
2. 厳格な家父長制社会であるアルバニアにもこのような習慣がある。
3. アルバニアの類似の慣習では、貞節を誓い、男であると宣言すれば財産を引き継ぐことができる。
4. アルバニアでは、通常女性が村議会の一員になることは許されていない。

Newspaper English

 英文記事では簡潔な表現が好まれるため、分詞構文が頻出します。分詞構文では接続詞や主語、be 動詞が省かれ、情報を簡潔に提示します。

1 と 2 の英文の下線部の接続詞節を分詞構文に書き換え、日本語訳を完成させましょう。

1. <u>Since they are dressed in</u> sweaters and jeans or the traditional Afghan male clothing of baggy pants and long shirt, none stand out as they jostle to score a goal.

→ [　　　　　　　　　　　　　　　　]

セーターにジーンズか、バギーパンツにロングシャツといった伝統的なアフガンの男性の服装

_____、男の子たちが押し合いへし合いしながらゴールを決める中、目立つものはいない。

2. <u>Although she is unbeknownst</u> to them, one is different from the others.

→ [　　　　　　　　　　　　　　　　]

彼らに_____、一人はそれ以外の子たちとは異なっている。

Reading

Afghan girls get to be boys, for limited time

KABUL — In a Kabul neighborhood, a gaggle of boys kick a yellow ball around a dusty playground, their boisterous cries echoing off the surrounding apartment buildings.

⁵ Dressed in sweaters and jeans or the traditional Afghan male clothing of baggy pants and long shirt, none stand out as they jostle to score a goal. But unbeknownst to them, one is different from the others.

At not quite 8 years old, Sanam is a bacha posh: a girl
¹⁰ living as a boy. One day a few months ago, the girl with rosy cheeks and an impish smile had her dark hair cut short, donned boys' clothes and took on a boy's name, Omid. The move opened up a boy's world: playing soccer and cricket with boys, wrestling with the neighborhood
¹⁵ butcher's son, working to help the family make ends meet.

In Afghanistan's heavily patriarchal, male-dominated society, where women and girls are usually relegated to the home, bacha posh, Dari for "dressed as a boy," is the one tradition allowing girls access to the freer male world.
²⁰ Under the practice, a girl dresses, behaves and is treated as a boy, with all the freedoms and obligations that entails. The child can play sports, attend a madrassa, or religious school, and, sometimes crucially for the family, work. But there is a time limit: Once a bacha posh reaches
²⁵ puberty, she is expected to revert to traditional girls' gender roles. The transition is not always easy.

It is unclear how the practice is viewed by Afghanistan's new rulers, the Taliban, who seized power in mid-August and have made no public statements on the issue.
³⁰ Their rule so far has been less draconian than the last time they were in power in the 1990s, but women's freedoms have still been severely curtailed. Thousands of women have been barred from working, and girls beyond primary school age have not been able to return to public
³⁵ schools in most places.

With a crackdown on women's rights, the bacha posh

Glossary (right margin):

gaggle「一団」

boisterous「騒がしい」

impish「いたずらな」

male-dominated「男性支配的な」

relegate... to ~「…を~に追いやる」

Dari「ダリー語（アフガニスタンの公用語の一つ）」

obligation「義務」

entail...「~を（必然的に）伴う」

madrassa「マドラサ（イスラム教の学校のこと）」

crucially「極めて重要なことに」

draconian「極めて厳格な」

curtail...「~を抑制する」

crackdown「弾圧、取り締まり」

tradition could become even more attractive for some families. And as the practice is temporary, with the children eventually reverting to female roles, the Taliban
40 might not deal with the issue at all, said Thomas Barfield, a professor of anthropology at Boston University who has written several books on Afghanistan.

anthropology「人類学」

"Because it's inside the family and because it's not a permanent status, the Taliban may stay out [of it],"
45 Barfield said.

The Associated Press

Comprehension

本文の内容に合うように、1と2の質問の答えとして適当なものを、3の英文の空所に入るものとして適当なものを、a〜dから選びましょう。

1. How has becoming a bacha posh changed Sanam's life?
    a. She is able to work in the local butcher's shop to support her family.
    b. Her new status allows her to avoid responsibilities in the home.
    c. She no longer has to wear colorful makeup on her face.
    d. For the time being, her name has been changed to Omid.

2. Which of the following is NOT mentioned as a freedom enjoyed by a bacha posh?
    a. The ability to get married to someone who they love
    b. The opportunity to work and earn money for their families
    c. The chance to play sports, such as soccer and cricket
    d. The option to attend classes at religious schools

3. Professor Thomas Barfield believes the Taliban may _____ the tradition of bacha posh.
    a. crack down severely on
    b. possibly ignore
    c. continue to curtail
    d. forbid

Summary

DL 24　　CD 1-40

以下の空所1〜4に当てはまる語を選択肢から選び、書き入れましょう。

A young Afghan girl has transitioned into a bacha posh, taking on the
(1.　　　　　　　　　) of a boy. In Afghanistan, participating in this
(2.　　　　　　　　　) means that girls can take on the role of boys
until they reach puberty. This allows them to enjoy many privileges,
including the opportunity to work and make money for their families. With
the Taliban's recent (3.　　　　　　　　　) to power and their policies
restricting women from working, this may be an appealing
(4.　　　　　　　) for families.

option　　tradition　　rise　　appearance

Insights into Today's World

DL 25　　CD 1-41

以下の対話の空所に、あなたの考えを書いてみましょう。その後、クラスメイトにその内容を伝えてみましょう。

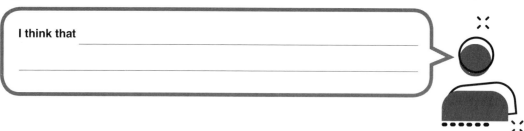

I'm very surprised to know that some Afghan girls are living as boys! I wonder what it would be like to live for a while as a person of a different gender. I have mixed feelings about it.
What do you think?

I think that _____

_____

Chapter 09

Buy a Drink, Change the World

自動販売機で社会貢献

Donation-type vending machines
(Courtesy of KY [left] / The Nippon Foundation [right])

Key Expressions 1

🎧 DL 26　　◉ CD 1-42

音声を聞いて 1 ～ 3 の（　　）内に適当な語を書き入れましょう。

1. There are about 4 (m _ _ _ _ _ _) vending machines dotted all over Japan.
   およそ 400 万台の自動販売機が日本の至る所に点在している。

2. When beverages are purchased from the vending machine, part of the amount
   paid is (a _ _ _ _ _ _ _ _ _ _ _ _ _) donated to charitable organizations.
   飲み物がその自動販売機で購入されると、支払われた額の一部が自動的に慈善団体に寄付される。

3. The vending machine market has (r _ _ _ _ _ _) a saturation point.
   自動販売機市場は飽和状態に達している。

Key Expressions 2

waiting room（待合室）などのように、「動名詞＋名詞」の形式では、動名詞が後に続く名詞の用途や目的を表します。

日本語訳を参考に、適当な動詞を選択肢から選び、1〜5の（　　）内に動名詞の形にして書き入れましょう。

1. (　　　　　　　　　　　) paper 　　　　　［包装紙］
2. (　　　　　　　　　　　) room 　　　　　［更衣室］
3. (　　　　　　　　　　　) machine 　　　［ミシン］
4. (　　　　　　　　　　　) machine 　　　［自動販売機］
5. metal (　　　　　　　　　　　) equipment 　　　［金属探知機］

vend　　change　　sew　　wrap　　detect

Key Expressions 3

日本語訳を参考に、have の使い方に注意して、1〜3の英文の（　　）内に当てはまる動詞を選択肢から選び、必要であれば形を変えて書き入れましょう。

1. Many vending machines have security cameras (　　　　　　　　　　　)
   and can alert the police if somebody tries to steal the contents.
   多くの自動販売機には防犯カメラが取り付けられていて、誰かが中身を盗もうとすれば警察に通報することができる。

2. This business model has the owners of vending machines
   (　　　　　　　　　　　) a portion of their sales proceeds to charitable
   organizations.
   このビジネスモデルでは、自動販売機のオーナーに収益の一部を慈善団体に寄付してもらう。

3. We would like to have a vending machine (　　　　　　　　　　　) with
   graphic art.
   私たちは、自動販売機をグラフィックアートでラッピングしてもらいたいと思っています。

donate　　wrap　　install

Background Knowledge

◎ CD 1-43

日本財団が 2020 年度に行ったことについて、英文に<u>述べられていないもの</u>を 1 〜 4 から選びましょう。

In fiscal 2020, the Nippon Foundation installed 486 new charity vending machines at social welfare organizations and other entities, bringing the total of charity vending machines to 8,110. The foundation donates ¥10 per bottle of beverage — funneling about ¥280 million to support children with intractable diseases and others in the same fiscal year alone.

The Japan News

Notes entity「組織、団体」 funnel...「（資金など）を送る」 intractable disease「難病」

1. 日本財団は 486 台のチャリティー自動販売機を設置した。
2. 日本財団の設置したチャリティー自動販売機の合計が 8,110 台になった。
3. 日本財団は、チャリティー自動販売機の収益から 280 万円を寄付した。
4. 日本財団からの寄付は、難病の子どもたちやその他の人々の支援のために送られた。

Newspaper English

英文記事では、数値に関する情報は重要です。「〜につき、〜あたり」の意味を表す前置詞 per もよく用いられます。900 yen per hour のように、〈数値に関する情報＋per＋単数名詞〉の形で表され、単数名詞は無冠詞である点に注意しましょう。

1 〜 3 の英文の（　　）内に当てはまる語を選択肢から選び、書き入れましょう。

1. We would like to consider donating more per (　　　　　　　　　) in the future.
   私たちは将来 1 本あたりの寄付を増やすことを検討したいと思います。

2. Japan has the highest number of vending machines per (　　　　　　) in the world.
   日本は 1 人あたりの自動販売機の数が世界で最も多い。

3. The average revenue for a vending machine is over $300 per (　　　　　　).
   1 台の自動販売機の平均収入は、ひと月あたり 300 ドルを超える。

month　　bottle　　capita

Reading

'Donation-type vending machines' are serving charity on Japan's streets

Japan's ubiquitous vending machines are now being tapped as a convenient way for consumers to change the world with their pocket change.

"Donation-type vending machines" have been popping
5 up on street corners in recent years, as a new business model that has owners donate a portion of their sales proceeds to charitable organizations.

Operators hope the initiative will be a win-win for both society and businesses, by providing consumers an added
10 incentive to select their machines over the many others in the vending machine capital of the world.

In September, Kazuki Hirose, the 42-year-old president of KY, an HVAC contractor in Yokohama, installed a charity vending machine on the first floor of his building.
15 "Neighbors have approached me to express their delight at being able to contribute to society [through the vending machine]," Hirose said.

The company has chosen to donate proceeds earned from the machine to Japan Team of Young Human Power
20 (JHP), a Tokyo-based nonprofit organization working to build schools mainly in Cambodia. Since the company has to foot the bill for electricity and other costs, the amount donated comes out to only ¥1 per bottle sold. But it has still attracted many supporters, including some who travel
25 long distances specifically to buy drinks from the machine.

The company received its SDGs (Sustainable Development Goals) accreditation from the city in June, and had been looking for additional ways to contribute to society.
30 "It's helped raise our company's profile," Hirose said. "We would like to consider donating more per bottle in the future."

Interest in charity vending machines is on the rise, according to a Tokyo nonprofit group that connects
35 charities with companies that want to participate in the

---

donation「寄付」

ubiquitous「至る所にある」
tap...「〜を活用する」
pocket change「（ポケットの中にあるくらいの）小銭」
pop up「出現する、現れる」

initiative「（新たな）取り組み」

incentive「インセンティブ、動機」

HVAC contractor「空調設備工事業者（HVAC は heating, ventilating, air conditioning の略）」
delight「喜び」

foot the bill「費用を負担する」
come out to...「〜という結果になる」
specifically「特に」

accreditation「認証評価」
contribute「貢献する」

raise one's profile「〜の認知度（注目度）を上げる」

on the rise「増えつつある」

---

initiative. The group said the number of charity vending machines it helped install tripled from about 80 in 2015 to about 270 in 2020.

triple「3倍になる」

To make donation-type machines stand out on the
40　street, they are wrapped with graphics advertising the name and activities of the charity in question. Beneficiaries of the system have said they are grateful for both the donations and the extra exposure.

The Japan News

stand out「目立つ、注目を浴びる」

in question「当該の」

beneficiary「受益者（ここでは寄付を受ける側）」

grateful「感謝して」

exposure「露出（注目を集めること）」

Comprehension

本文の内容に合うように、1と2の英文を完成させるのに適当なものを、3の質問の答えとして適当なものを、a～dから選びましょう。

1. Kazuki Hirose installed a charity vending machine in his company's building
   a. to improve his company's relationship with the neighbors.
   b. in order to draw customers to the building and increase profits.
   c. because he was searching for ways to give back to humanity.
   d. so that he could receive SDG certification from the Yokohama city government.

2. Kazuki Hirose's company donates only ¥1 per bottle sold from their charity vending machine because
   a. there are expenses related to the vending machine that they must pay.
   b. they have not yet attracted enough customers to the machine.
   c. that is the amount requested by the JHP non-profit organization.
   d. the company needs to increase its profile before considering an increase.

3. Which of the following is NOT likely to be found on a charity vending machine?
   a. Images depicting a charity's activities
   b. Artwork meant to attract customers' attention
   c. The name of the associated charity
   d. Details about the owner of the machine

Summary

DL 27   CD 1-45

以下の空所 1 ～ 4 に当てはまる語を選択肢から選び、必要であれば形を変えて書き入れましょう。

In Japan, an emerging business model that (1.　　　　　　　　　　　)
vending machine owners with charitable organizations has grown in
popularity in recent years. These charity vending machines
(2.　　　　　　　　　　　) companies to give to those less fortunate and
also (3.　　　　　　　　　　　) sympathetic customers who want to put
their money to a good cause. Though the percentage of the cost of each
beverage donated is small, charities (4.　　　　　　　　　　　) the
donations and the increased publicity.

allow   appreciate   attract   partner

Insights into Today's World

DL 28   CD 1-46

以下の対話の空所に、あなたのアイデアを書いてみましょう。その後、クラスメイトにその内容を伝えてみましょう。

It seems the number of charity vending machines has been increasing in recent
years. It's convenient to be able to make a small donation by simply buying a soft
drink. But I can't find any of them around here.
How do you think we can increase their number even more?

How about _____ ?
_____

Chapter 10

Real × Unreal

異次元ファッションへの試み

A dress designed by Kunihiko Morinaga (The Yomiuri Shimbun)

Key Expressions 1

🎧 DL 29　◎ CD 1-47

音声を聞いて 1 ～ 3 の（　　）内に適当な語を書き入れましょう。

1. The work of Kunihiko Morinaga is known for actively (i _ _ _ _ _ _ _ _ _ _ _)
the latest technology.

森永邦彦氏の作品は、最新のテクノロジーを積極的に取り入れることで知られている。

2. As part of Anrealage's entry for Paris Fashion Week Spring and Summer 2022,
digital fashion model avatars would appear and walk down a runway in the
(v _ _ _ _ _ _) space.

パリ・ファッションウィーク 2022 春夏の Anrealage（アンリアレイジ：森永氏の手がけるファッションブランド）
の参加の一環として、デジタルのファッションモデルのアバターたちが仮想空間に現れて、ランウェイを歩く。

3. The (g _ _ _ _ _ _ _) Morinaga designed, both digital and physical, can change
color in an instant when they are bathed in a flash of light.

森永氏のデジタルと実物の両方でデザインした服は、光を浴びると即座に色を変えることができる。

Key Expressions 2

1 ～ 5 は本文に使われている動詞です。それぞれの語に合う英英定義を a ～ e から選びましょう。

1. depict（描く） [   ]
2. emerge（現れる） [   ]
3. commission（委託する） [   ]
4. represent（表す） [   ]
5. showcase（披露する） [   ]

a. formally hire someone to do a specific job
b. come forth into view or notice, as from concealment
c. exhibit or display
d. be a sign or symbol of something
e. show something in a picture or story

Key Expressions 3

接続詞 when や while の節ではしばしば主語と be 動詞が省略されます。日本語訳を参考に、1 ～ 3 の [   ] 内の語句を適当な順番に並び替えましょう。

1. His clothing includes resin materials that change color [to / ultraviolet light / exposed / when] .
   彼の服は、紫外線にさらされると色が変わる樹脂素材を含んでいる。

   _____

2. He designed clothing with colors and patterns that emerge [illuminated / a flashlight / with / when] .
   彼は、フラッシュの光で照らされると現れる色や模様の服をデザインした。

   _____

3. Morinaga has been experimenting with the latest technology [various industries / collaborating / while / in / with people] .
   森永氏は、様々な業界の人たちとコラボしながら、最新のテクノロジーを用いて実験をしてきた。

   _____

Background Knowledge

CD 1-48

森永邦彦氏のファッションブランド Anrealage（アンリアレイジ）の作品とデジタル
テクノロジーについて、英文に<u>述べられていないもの</u>を 1 ～ 4 から選びましょう。

　Incorporating digital technology has become a notable topic in the fashion
industry. The brand's latest online collection has surpassed even Morinaga's
expectations, garnering more than 1 million views. He has even received inquiries
from entities such as The Metropolitan Museum of Art in New York.

　As a new project, the brand has sold the works based on the Belle collaboration
as nonfungible tokens (NFTs). This refers to digital data authenticated by
blockchain technology, which is known for its role in cryptocurrency systems, as
being unique and non-interchangeable.

The Japan News

Notes　garner...「～を獲得する」　the Belle collaboration「アニメ『竜とそばかすの姫』の主人公ベルをモチーフにした
コラボ商品」　nonfungible token「非代替性トークン（NFT）」　cryptocurrency「暗号通貨（仮想通貨の一種）」

1. ファッションにデジタルテクノロジーを取り入れる動きは今までなかった。
2. 森永氏の最新のコレクションのオンラインでの披露は予想を上回る視聴回数となった。
3. アンリアレイジはアニメとのコラボ作品を NFT として販売している。
4. NFT とは、ブロックチェーン技術によって認証を受けた、唯一無二で交換不可能なデジタル
　 データのことである。

Newspaper English

 近年発展がめざましいデジタルテクノロジー分野の記事においては、聞き慣れない用語や
新しい会社・組織の名前がしばしば登場します。それらには詳しい説明が補足されている
こともあり、物事を説明する表現や言い換えの技法を学ぶ良い機会を与えてくれます。

以下の英文の（　　）内に当てはまる語を選択肢から選び、書き入れましょう。

Morinaga established Anrealage in 2003; the name being a combination of
"(　　　　　　　　　　　　　)" to represent the ordinary, "(　　　　　　　　　　　　　)"
for the extraordinary, and "(　　　　　　　　　　　　　)" to express an era.

age　　　unreal　　　real

Anime x Paris Fashion Week / Anrealage's online collection opens up whole new world

Japanese fashion brand Anrealage's entry for Paris Fashion Week for Spring and Summer 2022, which incorporated aspects of Mamoru Hosoda's latest animated film "Ryu to Sobakasu no Hime" (Belle), made the label a hot topic.

The work of founder Kunihiko Morinaga, much like the film, is also known to actively incorporate the latest technology.

During the show, digital fashion model avatars would appear and walk down a runway in the virtual space depicted in the film. Live models would then take the stage, appearing to have emerged from the screen, wearing the same ensembles.

Morinaga designed the garments, both digital and physical, with combinations of triangular patterns and an ability to change color in an instant when bathed in a flash of light.

The collaboration between Morinaga and Hosoda began when the filmmaker commissioned a dress design for Belle, the film's eponymous heroine, from Morinaga.

"There's more freedom when it comes to designing animated clothes rather than ordinary ones. I was even able to change their colors every second," Morinaga said. "I worked with the idea that even though [the clothes] had no physical form, the fashion itself would be sure to leave an impression. It was a fresh and interesting experience for me."

Morinaga established Anrealage in 2003; the name being a combination of "real" to represent the ordinary, "unreal" for the extraordinary, and "age" to express an era.

As the name may suggest, Morinaga has been experimenting with the latest technology, which has yet to become a part of everyday life, and collaborating with people in various industries.

Clothing that includes resin materials that change color

aspect「要素」
label「ブランド」

ensemble「アンサンブル（服の組み合わせのこと）」

commission... from ~「～（人）に…（作品など）を委託する」
eponymous「作品のタイトルとなっている」

impression「印象」

when exposed to ultraviolet light or clothing with colors and patterns that emerge when illuminated with a flashlight are just some of the fruits of his endeavors.

fruit「成果」

40 Although Anrealage has been taking part in Paris Fashion Week since 2014, some of the brand's recent collections have been showcased online due to the novel coronavirus pandemic.

endeavor「試み」

"Digital presentations are completely different from live shows," Morinaga said. "Where live shows are given for 45 audiences with a limited number of people, digital shows allow everyone to view [the collections] objectively. [Digital shows] can become an opportunity to create new emotions and experiences."

objectively「客観的に」

The Japan News

Comprehension

本文の内容に合うように、1と2の質問の答えとして適当なものを、3の英文を完成させるのに適当なものを、a〜dから選びましょう。

1. Which element was NOT included in the Anrealage show at Paris Fashion Week for Spring and Summer 2022?
   a. Clothing designs that include an arrangement of triangles
   b. Physically present models wearing clothes that were designed by Hosoda
   c. The depiction of a virtual space from the film, Belle
   d. Digital avatars modeling garments that respond to light

2. According to Morinaga, what is the advantage of designing animated clothes over physical clothes?
   a. There is a greater sense of collaboration.
   b. Physical clothes are too ordinary.
   c. Physical garments leave a stronger impression on the viewer.
   d. There are fewer limitations placed on the designer.

3. Morinaga
   a. believes that online fashion shows have certain advantages.
   b. tends to use conventional materials when designing clothes.
   c. has had a working relationship with Mamoru Hosoda since 2003.
   d. began his career by designing clothing for animated films.

Summary

DL 30　CD 1-50

以下の空所 1 〜 4 に当てはまる語を選択肢から選び、書き入れましょう。

Japanese fashion designer, Kunihiko Morinaga, uses his Anrealage brand to blur the boundaries between (1.　　　　　　　　　) fashion and various seemingly (2.　　　　　　　　　) industries. He recently unveiled the results of a collaboration with filmmaker Mamoru Hosoda at Paris Fashion Week, which combined real and (3.　　　　　　　　　) elements. In response to the coronavirus pandemic, the brand has begun to showcase its collections digitally, sharing Morinaga's vision with a (4.　　　　　　　　　) audience.

wider　　high　　unrelated　　virtual

Insights into Today's World

DL 31　CD 1-51

以下の対話の空所に、あなたの考えを書いてみましょう。その後、クラスメイトにその内容を伝えてみましょう。

Morinaga's collection is revolutionary! He collaborated with the famous animated film director, Mamoru Hosoda, and created such fantastical clothing. The sense of unreality makes his fashion unique. I think it is a good idea to incorporate the latest technology into fashion.
Do you want to wear clothes like this?

In my case, _____

_____

Tiny Organisms Play a Big Role

ミクロの生物、生態系を揺るがす

Scientist Clare Ostle (AFP-JIJI)

Key Expressions 1

🎧 DL 32　◎ CD 2-02

音声を聞いて 1 ～ 3 の（　　）内に適当な語を書き入れましょう。

1. Scientist Clare Ostle poses (a _ _ _ _ _ _ _ _) a continuous plankton recorder (CPR) on a research vessel.

   科学者のクレア・オストル氏が、調査船上で、連続プランクトン採集器（CPR）と並んでポーズをとっている。

2. According to Ostle, conservation has focused on the big things, the cute things and the things that are directly worth money like whales, turtles and cod, but they all (r _ _ _) on plankton.

   オストル氏によると、これまで自然保護は、クジラやウミガメ、タラなど、大きなものやかわいいもの、直接お金になるものに焦点を当ててきたが、これらはすべてプランクトンに依存している。

3. Although plankton are microscopic, people can see (t _ _ _ _ _) of them at the beach — in foam on waves or the nighttime twinkle of bioluminescence.

   プランクトンは微細なものだが、それらの痕跡は、波の泡や夜の生物発光のきらめきとして、海岸で見ることができる。

Key Expressions 2

1 〜 5 は接尾辞 -al を伴った形容詞です。日本語訳を参考に、それぞれの英英定義を a 〜 e から選び、その記号を（　）内に書き入れましょう。

1. crucial　　　　［重大な、危機的な］　　　（　　　　）
2. biological　　　［生物の、生物学の］　　　（　　　　）
3. global　　　　　［地球（規模）の］　　　　（　　　　）
4. potential　　　［可能性のある］　　　　　（　　　　）
5. seasonal　　　　［季節の］　　　　　　　　（　　　　）

　　　　a. relating to living things
　　　　b. possible or likely in the future
　　　　c. extremely important
　　　　d. affecting the whole world
　　　　e. characteristic of a particular time of the year

Key Expressions 3

that 節の代表的な働きとして以下の 1 〜 3 があります。それぞれの説明を参考にして、that 節の日本語訳を完成させましょう。

1. 名詞節として、主語・目的語・補語になる節を導く

What the researchers have seen is that as climate change heats the seas, plankton are on the move.

これまで研究者たちが見てきたのは、_____

_____。

2. 形容詞節として、名詞の直後に続いて名詞を修飾する

Plankton are part of an intricately balanced system that helps keep us all alive.

プランクトンは、_____

複雑に均衡がとれた生態系の一部である。

3. 副詞節として、形容詞や副詞の後ろに続きそれらを修飾する

The big worry is when change happens so quickly that the ecosystem can't recover.

大きな懸念は、_____ほど早く変化が起きるときである。

Background Knowledge CD 2-03

植物プランクトンの働きについて、英文に述べられているものを 1 ～ 4 から選びましょう。

Phytoplankton photosynthesize using the sun's rays to turn carbon dioxide into energy and oxygen. In fact, scientists estimate that the seas produce around half the oxygen on Earth, and that is mostly thanks to phytoplankton. They are also crucial to the ocean's "biological carbon pump," which helps the sea lock away at least a quarter of carbon dioxide emitted by burning fossil fuels.

While trees store carbon in wood and leaves, phytoplankton store it in their bodies. It passes through the food web, with phytoplankton consumed by zooplankton, which, in turn, are eaten by creatures ranging from birds to whales.

AFP -JIJI

Note　photosynthesize「光合成する」

1. 太陽エネルギーを二酸化炭素に変換している。
2. 海が地球上の酸素の約半分を生産するのを支えている。
3. 化石燃料を採掘するときに排出される二酸化炭素を植物の中に閉じ込める。
4. 鳥やクジラのえさになっている。

Newspaper English

専門知識を必要とする内容の新聞記事では、専門用語の後ろにダッシュ（―）やコンマ（,）で区切った用語の説明が付けられることがしばしばあり、読者の理解を助けています。

1 ～ 4 の空所に日本語を書き入れ、英文中の下線部の語句の説明を完成させましょう。

This is a <u>continuous plankton recorder (CPR)</u>, a torpedo-like device that for 90 years has been towed by merchant vessels and fishing boats on a vast network of routes.

これは、「連続プランクトン採集器（CPR）」で、90 年にわたって、広大なネットワークの航路上の
1.＿＿＿＿＿＿＿や 2.＿＿＿＿＿＿＿によって牽引されてきた魚雷の形に似た 3.＿＿＿＿＿＿＿である。

<u>Plankton</u> — organisms carried on the tides — are the foundation of the marine food web.
4.＿＿＿＿＿＿＿＿＿＿＿に乗って運ばれる生物であるプランクトンは、海洋の食物網の基盤である。

Reading

Drifting into trouble? The tiny ocean creatures with a global impact

drift into... 「〜に巻き込まれる」

The strange metal box hauled from the waves and onto the ship's deck looks like a spaceship fished from a child's imagination.

haul... 「〜を引き上げる」

5 But when scientist Clare Ostle opens it up and draws out the silk scrolls inside, she is looking for the telltale green glow from some of the most important creatures on Earth: plankton.

scroll「巻物」
telltale「証拠の」

This is a continuous plankton recorder (CPR), a torpedo-like device that for 90 years has been towed by merchant
10 vessels and fishing boats on a vast network of routes.

These recorders help researchers better understand the ocean by collecting some of its smallest inhabitants.

inhabitant「住人」

What they have seen is that as climate change heats the seas, plankton are on the move — with potentially
15 profound consequences for both ocean life and humans.

profound「深刻な、重大な」
consequence「結果」

Plankton — organisms carried on the tides — are the foundation of the marine food web. But they are also part of an intricately balanced system that helps keep us all alive.

20 As well as helping produce much of the oxygen we breathe, they are a crucial part of the global carbon cycle.

breathe「呼吸する」

"The big thing that we're seeing is warming," Ostle, coordinator of the Pacific CPR Survey, says as she demonstrates the plankton recorder off the coast of
25 Plymouth in Britain.

off the coast of... 「〜沖で」

The CPR Survey has documented a decisive shift of plankton toward both the poles in recent decades as ocean currents change and many marine animals head for cooler areas.

document... 「〜を記録する」
decisive「明らかな」
the poles「極（南極と北極）」
ocean current「海流」

30 Smaller warm water plankton are also replacing more nutritious cold water ones, often also with differing seasonal cycles, meaning the species that feed on them need to adapt or move too.

replace... 「〜に置き換わる、〜に取って代わる」
nutritious「栄養価の高い」
feed on... 「〜を餌にする」
adapt... 「〜に適応する」

"The big worry is when change happens so quickly that
35 the ecosystem can't recover," says Ostle, adding that

dramatic temperature spikes can lead "whole fisheries to collapse."

With nearly half of humanity reliant on fish for some 20% of their animal protein, this could be devastating.

40 Average global phytoplankton biomass — a measure of total weight or quantity — is predicted to fall by around 1.8% to 6%, depending on the level of greenhouse gas emissions.

But because of its outsized importance, even modest
45 reductions can "amplify up the marine food web," eventually leading to reductions in marine life by roughly 5% to 17%.

AFP -JIJI

spike	「急上昇」
fishery	「水産業」
collapse	「崩壊する」
reliant on...	「～に依存している」
devastating	「壊滅的な」
biomass	「（生物）量」
outsized	「特大の」
modest	「少しの、緩やかな」
reduction	「減少」
amplify up...	「～を増幅させる」
eventually	「最終的には」

● Comprehension

本文の内容に合うように、1 の英文を完成させるのに適当なものを、2 と 3 の質問の答えとして適当なものを、a～d から選びましょう。

1. According to Clare Ostle, the most significant concern is
   a. the absence of a green glow in the continuous plankton recorder (CPR).
   b. changes to the ocean's ecosystems caused by rapid temperature increases.
   c. a decrease in the amount of carbon produced by plankton.
   d. dramatic dips in the temperature of the Earth's oceans.

2. Which does NOT describe the purpose of a continuous plankton recorder?
   a. To track the location of the ocean's plankton
   b. To collect plankton for researchers to analyze
   c. To examine how plankton are impacted by merchant ships
   d. To carry silk scrolls that exhibit evidence of plankton

3. How might changes in the ocean's ecosystems affect humans?
   a. Marine species people consume won't have access to the more nutritious plankton found in cold water.
   b. The fishing industry might see a 20% drop in the number of fish they catch.
   c. Many people would experience an increase in the amount of protein in their diets.
   d. Humanity may be forced to migrate closer to the poles to avoid warm water.

Summary

DL 33　CD 2-05

以下の空所 1 〜 4 に当てはまる語を選択肢から選び、書き入れましょう。

> As the Earth's climate continues to ($^{1.}$), researchers have discovered that the warming seas are having a negative impact on plankton, organisms which ($^{2.}$) the base of the oceans' food web and are the source of much of the world's oxygen. Effects ($^{3.}$) shifts in habitat and life cycles. This could lead to potentially disastrous consequences for sea life and the humans that ($^{4.}$) on it.

change　　form　　rely　　include

Insights into Today's World

DL 34　CD 2-06

以下の対話の空所に、あなたの試みを書いてみましょう。その後、クラスメイトにその内容を伝えてみましょう。

It was surprising that plankton are so small, yet they sustain life on earth. We humans must make efforts to stop global warming and protect the marine environment in which they live.
What steps are you taking to protect marine life?

Well, _____

_____

Chapter 12

Amateurs Beat Professionals at their Own Game

素人アイデアが革新を産む?!

A photo taken by a participant in a cognitive science study (Provided by Kazuhiro Ueda)

Key Expressions 1

 DL 35　 CD 2-07

音声を聞いて 1 〜 3 の（　　）内に適当な語を書き入れましょう。

1. In an experiment, participants were asked to take a picture of their own speaker and come up with an idea for a new (f _ _ _ _ _ _ _) for the audio device.

   ある実験で、参加者たちは自分のスピーカーの写真を撮影し、そのオーディオ機器の新機能のアイデア
   を出すように求められた。

2. According to a cognitive science study, expert knowledge might be a hindrance to (c _ _ _ _ _ _ _) thinking.

   認知科学に関するある研究によると、専門知識は創造的思考の妨げになる可能性がある。

3. Non-professionals may think more freely compared to (t _ _ _ _) with more professional knowledge.

   素人は、より専門的な知識を持った人に比べてより自由に思考するのかもしれない。

Key Expressions 2

形容詞に -ly を足すことで副詞を形成します。形容詞が名詞を修飾するのに対し、副詞は動詞、形容詞、文全体などを修飾します。-ly を足す場合の語尾の変化に注意しましょう。

枠内の説明を参考に 1 〜 5 の形容詞を副詞に書き換え、その意味を選択肢から選び、書き入れましょう。解答例：free → (freely) ［自由に］

1. converse　　→ (　　　　　　　　　　　　　　) [　　　　　　　　]
2. active　　　→ (　　　　　　　　　　　　　　) [　　　　　　　　]
3. sole　　　　→ (　　　　　　　　　　　　　　) [　　　　　　　　]
4. relative　　→ (　　　　　　　　　　　　　　) [　　　　　　　　]
5. statistic　　→ (　　　　　　　　　　　　　　) [　　　　　　　　]

> 積極的に　　　逆に　　　統計的に　　　比較的・相対的に　　　〜だけに、単に

Key Expressions 3

以下は、科学研究を紹介する記事に頻出する表現を含む英文です。日本語訳を参考に、1 〜 4 の（　　　　）内に当てはまる動詞を選択肢から選び、適当な形に変化させて書き入れましょう。

1. A group of researchers (　　　　　　　　　　) that participants with less professional knowledge fared better when asked for ideas.

   ある研究者グループが、アイデアを求められた場合、専門的な知識が少ない（研究）参加者の方がうまくやることを示した。

2. Two hundred participants were (　　　　　　　　) about their professional knowledge related to engineering and acoustics.

   200 人の参加者が、工学と音響学に関する自身の専門知識について問われた。

3. As a result, they (　　　　　　　　　) that many participants with more professional knowledge could not come up with an idea for a new function.

   その結果、専門的な知識を多く持つ参加者の多くが、新機能のアイデアを思いつくことができないことがわかった。

4. The findings were recently (　　　　　　　　　) in *Scientific Reports*.

   本研究成果は、最近『サイエンティフィック・リポーツ』誌に掲載された。

Note　*Scientific Reports*: ネイチャー・リサーチ社刊行のオンラインでオープンアクセスの電子ジャーナル

> ask　　publish　　find　　show

Background Knowledge

CD 2-08

『サイエンティフィック・リポーツ』誌に掲載されたある論文の要旨について、英文に述べられているものを 1 ～ 4 から選びましょう。

　Many studies have suggested that creative activities are essential for social innovation. According to a paper published in *Scientific Reports*, people with less specialized knowledge tend to pay divided attention when processing information, which has a positive impact on their creative performance. Conversely, those with more expertise tend to pay more focused attention, which has a negative impact on their performance. The findings of this research will contribute to the real world by suggesting new ways of utilizing ideas from non-professionals to achieve innovations.

参考：https://www.nature.com/articles/s41598-021-97215-5

Notes innovation「変革」 expertise「専門知識」

1. 人が情報を処理する際、専門知識が豊富なほど的確に処理できる。
2. 人が情報を処理する際、知識量は情報処理のスピードには無関係である。
3. 専門知識の少ないことが、創造的なパフォーマンスにプラスの影響を与えうる。
4. 専門知識の多いことで注意力が散漫になると、創造的なパフォーマンスが低下する。

Newspaper English

 科学研究を紹介する記事において、当該研究を行った研究者のコメントがしばしば掲載されます。研究のアピール点を一般読者に訴えかける役割を果たします。

以下の英文は、Background Knowledge で取り上げた研究論文の著者のコメントです。研究要旨を参考にして、コメント内の 1 と 2 の空所に当てはまる語の組み合わせを a ～ d から選びましょう。

"[　1　] knowledge is important, of course. But in the initial process of coming up with an idea, people with [　2　] professional knowledge may be able to actively participate."

	1 に入る語	2 に入る語
a.	Professional	more
b.	Professional	less
c.	Non-professional	more
d.	Non-professional	less

Reading

Study: More expert knowledge a hindrance to creative thinking

hindrance「妨げ」

In some creative endeavors, the more professional knowledge people have, the more likely they will have tunnel vision and less likely to formulate a free and superior idea, a new study shows.

endeavor「試み、努力」
more likely「可能性が高い」
tunnel vision「トンネルビジョン」
formulate...「～を考案する」
superior「優れた」

5 A group of researchers, led by Kazuhiro Ueda, a professor of cognitive science at the University of Tokyo, showed that participants with less professional knowledge fared better when asked for ideas on improving the performance of an item in question.

in question「対象となっている」

10 "Professional knowledge is important, of course," Ueda said. "But in the initial process of putting an idea out, people with less professional knowledge may be able to actively participate."

The findings were recently published online in *Scientific*
15 *Reports*.

The researchers asked 200 participants about their professional knowledge pertaining to engineering and acoustics, specifically using stereo and computer speakers. The participants were also asked to take a picture of their
20 own speaker and come up with an idea of a new function for the audio device. The researchers processed these images to see where the participants' attention was focused. They also asked acoustic technology experts to evaluate the participants' ideas for a new function. The
25 researchers also analyzed tendencies by using a computing natural language processing technique.

pertaining to...「～に関する」
specifically「具体的に」

process...「～を処理する」

evaluate...「～を評価する」

As a result, they found a tendency for participants with more professional knowledge to focus on the details and concentrate their attention solely on the object.

30 Many such participants "could not come up with an idea" for a new function and proposed existing ideas, such as downsizing and making them higher quality. A statistical analysis showed that the concentrated attention had a negative effect on the quality of their ideas, the
35 researchers said.

existing「従来型の、既存の」
downsize「小型化する」

On the other hand, those with less professional knowledge tended to divide their attention and not focus solely on the device. They tended to come up with ideas that experts valued relatively highly, such as a "speaker
40 built into a book or a magazine." Dividing their attention on the problem at hand had a positive effect on their thinking, the researchers said.

value... 「〜を評価する」

at hand 「身近にある」

Those with more professional knowledge may tend to take a narrow look, while non-professionals may have a
45 wide breadth of vision and think freely.

Similar tendencies were found in a survey targeting more than 200,000 reviews of speakers sold on the online retailer Amazon, Ueda said.

online retailer 「インターネット通販業者」

The Asahi Shimbun Asia & Japan Watch

参考

tunnel vision (l. 3) 「トンネルビジョン」：トンネルの中で明るい出口だけを見るような、視野が狭まった状態を表す隠喩。

● **Comprehension**

本文の内容に合うように、1 と 3 の英文を完成させるのに適当なものを、2 の質問の答えとして適当なものを、a 〜 d から選びましょう。

1. The survey analysis results seem to suggest that

   a. deep knowledge is required to think critically about a topic.

   b. professionals are always effective thinkers.

   c. those with non-professional knowledge can play a role in improving products.

   d. experts do not tend to value original ideas.

2. Why were survey respondents asked to take photos of their audio equipment?

   a. For researchers to measure the degree of their concentration

   b. To get a sense of their knowledge about acoustics

   c. For researchers to see where participants direct their attention

   d. To understand which features of the speaker they actually use

3. According to the article, an example of a highly rated idea was a speaker that

    a. is reduced in size.

    b. has improved quality.

    c. is divided into multiple parts.

    d. is imbedded in a book.

Summary

 DL 36   CD 2-10

以下の空所 1 ～ 4 に当てはまる語を選択肢から選び、書き入れましょう。

> According to the results of a survey (¹.　　　　　　　　　) by a team
> of cognitive science researchers, individuals with (².　　　　　　　　)
> knowledge of a subject are not necessarily the best performers when it comes
> to original thinking about that topic. The study (³.　　　　　　　)
> that people with less specific knowledge seem to be more competent at taking
> a wider view and thinking "outside the box" when (⁴.　　　　　　　)
> to produce innovative ideas.

      asked   conducted   specialized   showed

Insights into Today's World

 DL 37   CD 2-11

以下の対話の空所に、あなたのアイデアを書いてみましょう。その後、クラスメイトにその内容を伝えてみましょう。

A research article published in *Scientific Reports* showed people with less professional knowledge might be able to actively participate in the process of producing ideas.
What is your advice for coming up with creative ideas?

I suggest _____

_____

Teaching Traditional Buddhism with Jokes

現代社会における宗教の在り方

A scene from a chat show in a Buddhist temple (Reuters/Aflo)

Key Expressions 1

🎧 DL 38　◎ CD 2-12

音声を聞いて 1 〜 3 の（　）内に適当な語を書き入れましょう。

1. Two Buddhist (m _ _ _ _) hosted a chat show during a Facebook live stream from a temple in Bangkok.

   2人の僧侶が、バンコクの寺院から、フェイスブックのライブ配信でチャットショーを主催した。

2. The live streams by the monks were a mixture of (t _ _ _ _ _ _ _ _ _) Buddhist teachings and jokes.

   僧侶らによるライブ配信は、伝統的な仏教の教えとジョークが混ざったものであった。

3. There are pros and cons for both creating a new style of Buddhism and protecting a (c _ _ _ _ _ _ _) style of Buddhism.

   新たな仏教のスタイルを作ることと古典的な仏教のスタイルを守ることの両方には、賛否両論がある。

Key Expressions 2

英単語を英英辞典で調べて英語での定義を確認すると、その単語の持つ微細なニュアンスも理解することができます。

以下の1～5は本文に出てくる語句です。英英定義をa～eの選択肢から選びましょう。

1. social media   [   ]
2. giggle   [   ]
3. slang   [   ]
4. decorum   [   ]
5. robe   [   ]

    a. laughing in an excited or silly way because something is funny

    b. formal behavior that shows respect and is considered appropriate for a particular situation

    c. platform for sharing information, opinions, images, videos, etc. using the Internet

    d. a long loose piece of clothing

    e. very informal language

Key Expressions 3

日本語訳を参考に、1～3の（　　）内に当てはまる語句を選択肢から選び、必要であれば形を変えて書き入れましょう。

1. Without (   ) the young, what will be the place of religion in the future?

   若者に働きかけることをしなければ、将来どこが宗教の場所となるのでしょうか。

2. Some Buddhist conservatives (   ) uphold the religion's conventions and formalities.

   仏教の保守派の中には、宗教のしきたりや形式を熱心に維持したがっている人もいる。

3. "That will (   ) the decline of Buddhism," said Srisuwan Janya.

   「それは、仏教の衰退につながるでしょう」とスリスワン・ジャンヤ氏が言った。

be keen to   lead to   reach out to

Background Knowledge

CD 2-13

タイの 2 人の僧侶、パイワン氏とソンポン氏が主催するライブ配信とそれに関連する事柄について、英文に<u>述べられていない</u>ものを 1 〜 4 から選びましょう。

　The live streams allow the two Buddhist monks to engage directly with their audience, reading comments and answering questions, a tactic that breaks the long-standing Buddhist convention of one-way preaching. In a recent live stream they riffed on the concept of "merits" and whether they could be shared.

　"Lord Buddha said merits are like candles," said Paiwan. "You can light other candles without dimming the flame of the first." Sompong, who has 1.4 million followers on Facebook, chimed in, "Just be careful not to burn your friends." Both men burst into giggles.

Reuters

Notes　tactic「手段」　riff「（気の利いたことを即座に）述べる」　merit「功徳」　dim...「〜を弱らせる」　chime in「（相手に合わせて）言う」

1. 2 人の僧侶は、ライブ配信中に答えられなかった質問には後日目を通して回答している。
2. 仏教の説教のスタイルは、長年、一方通行のものであった。
3. パイワン氏によると、お釈迦さまは功徳をロウソクに例えた。
4. ソンポン氏は、フェイスブックに 140 万人のフォロワーを持っている。

Newspaper English

英文記事の中で、人物のコメントは直接話法でよく紹介されます。直接話法を間接話法に書き換える際の主なステップは、次の通りです。

①主節の動詞を伝達動詞（tell, ask など）に変える
②被伝達部を that 節に変える
③被伝達部の中に使われる代名詞を適切なものにする
④被伝達部の動詞の時制を適切な形にする

例：He said to her, "I'm going to Tokyo." → He told her that he was going to Tokyo.

1 と 2 の直接話法の英文を間接話法に書き換えましょう。

1. Mr. Paiwan said to them, "I want Dhamma and young people to coexist."

　→ Mr. Paiwan _____.

2. A monk said to me, "My behavior has to be respectable."

　→ A monk _____.

Reading

Thai monks' live stream mixes Buddhism, jokes

Two Buddhist monks in Thailand have become social media stars with Facebook live streams that combine traditional teachings with non-traditional jokes and giggles. Some of the country's religious conservatives,
5 however, are not so amused.

With an impressive fluency in youth slang, Phra Maha Paiwan Warawanno, 30, and Phra Maha Sompong Talaputto, 42, have captured the imagination of a generation who find the formal temple decorum and
10 Sanskrit chanting of traditional Buddhism outdated and inaccessible.

On a recent Friday night, the bespectacled Paiwan set his phone up on a tripod and clipped a microphone onto his saffron robe, sitting alongside Phra Maha Sompong in
15 a small study in Wat Soi Thong temple in Bangkok. In the live stream that followed, the two men talked through a myriad of issues, mixing Buddhist teachings, known as Dhamma, with modern life advice and a hefty dose of humor.

20 "I want Dhamma and the young generation to coexist," said Paiwan. "Without reaching out to the young, what will be the place of religion in the future?" Paiwan and Sompong's weekly live streams attract hundreds of thousands of viewers within minutes, once reaching a
25 peak of 2 million. The upbeat sessions provided much-needed relief for many Thais confined to home during nighttime curfews to stifle the country's COVID-19 outbreak.

But the weekly live streams have not been greeted so
30 favorably by Buddhist conservatives keen to uphold the religion's conventions and formalities. The two monks were summoned last month to a parliamentary committee on religion to explain their online activities, while senior government figures have warned them to tone down the
35 jokes and "inappropriate behavior."

"Monks' behavior has to be respectable in the public eye.

---

religious「宗教的な」
amuse...「〜を面白がらせる」
impressive「見事な」
fluency「流暢さ」
capture the imagination of...
「〜の心を捉える」
Sanskrit「梵語、サンスクリット」
chanting「唱えること」
outdated「時代遅れの」
inaccessible「近づきにくい」
bespectacled「眼鏡をかけた」
tripod「三脚」
saffron「サフラン色の、鮮黄色の」
study「書斎」
a myriad of...「様々な、無数の〜」
a hefty dose of...「たくさんの〜」
upbeat「明るい、陽気な」
confine... to 〜「…を〜に閉じ込める」
curfew「外出禁止時間」
stifle...「〜を抑える」
outbreak「流行、(大量)発生」
favorably「好意的に」
summon...「〜を召喚する」
parliamentary「議会の」
senior government figure「政府高官」

It doesn't have to change with the time to appease young people," said Srisuwan Janya, head of the Association for the Protection of the Constitution. "That will lead to the
40 decline of Buddhism, which has already existed for nearly 2,600 years without needing to change before."

Paiwan responded with typical levity when asked to comment on the summons, "Laughing has become a national problem!"

45

Reuters

appease... 「～をなだめる」

the Association for the Protection of the Constitution 「憲法保護協会」

levity 「軽妙さ」

● **Comprehension**

本文の内容に合うように、1と3の質問の答えとして適当なものを、2の英文を完成させるのに適当なものを、a～dから選びましょう。

1. Which is least likely to be a feature of Paiwan and Sompong's live stream?
   a. Humorous commentary
   b. Tips on navigating modern life
   c. A variety of Sanskrit chants
   d. Buddhist teachings known as Dhamma

2. Traditional Buddhism is said to be unappealing to younger generations because
   a. the saffron robes worn by monks are unfashionable.
   b. decorations at temples have not been updated.
   c. some practices seem out of date.
   d. the monks tend to be too serious.

3. Which word best describes Srisuwan Janya's attitude toward Paiwan and Sompong's behavior?
   a. Supportive
   b. Critical
   c. Respectful
   d. Playful

Summary

DL 39　CD 2-15

以下の空所 1 ～ 4 に当てはまる語を選択肢から選び、書き入れましょう。

In an effort to reach a younger generation in the era of COVID-19, two Thai Buddhist monks live stream a (1.　　　　　　　　　) talk show that has become a hit on social media. Using an informal approach, including jokes and slang, the hosts share (2.　　　　　　　　　) Buddhist teachings in a (3.　　　　　　　　　) way. However, their tactics have met with (4.　　　　　　　　　) criticism from conservative-leaning members of the Buddhist community in Thailand.

traditional　　novel　　harsh　　weekly

Insights into Today's World

DL 40　CD 2-16

以下の対話の空所に、あなたの意見を書いてみましょう。その後、クラスメイトにその内容を伝えてみましょう。

Two Buddhist monks are working to share the teachings of Buddhism in a new style using social media, but there have been both positive and negative reactions.
What stance do you take? For or against? Why?

I take a stance for/against _____

_____

088

Chapter 14

Placing Hope in a Space Telescope

宇宙望遠鏡に託された期待

Ariane 5 rocket with NASA's James Webb Space Telescope (AFP-JIJI)

Key Expressions 1

🎧 DL 41　◎ CD 2-17

音声を聞いて 1 〜 3 の（　　）内に適当な語を書き入れましょう。

1. NASA's James Webb Space (T _ _ _ _ _ _ _ _) soared from French Guiana on South America's northeastern coast.

   アメリカ航空宇宙局（NASA）のジェームス・ウェッブ宇宙望遠鏡が、南アメリカ北東部沿岸のフランス領ギアナから舞い上がった。

2. "Webb will look back 13.7 (b _ _ _ _ _ _) years to when the first galaxies were born in the Universe," says NASA.

   「ウェッブは、宇宙で最初の銀河が誕生した137億年前まで振り返るでしょう」とNASAは言う。

3. NASA is shooting for 10 years of (o _ _ _ _ _ _ _ _ _ _) life from Webb.

   NASAは、ウェッブの運用寿命を10年とすることを目標にしている。

Key Expressions 2

1 〜 5 は宇宙科学の分野でよく見られる用語です。日本語に当てはまる語を選択肢から選び、（　）内に書き入れましょう。

1. 観測装置、天文台　　（　　　　　　　　　　　　　　）
2. 宇宙　　　　　　　　（　　　　　　　　　　　　　　）
3. 打ち上げ　　　　　　（　　　　　　　　　　　　　　）
4. 後継機、後継者　　　（　　　　　　　　　　　　　　）
5. 天文学者　　　　　　（　　　　　　　　　　　　　　）

cosmos　　successor　　observatory　　astronomer　　liftoff

Key Expressions 3

複数の語がハイフンでつながれて 1 つの形容詞の役割となるものを「複合形容詞」と呼びます。日本語訳を参考に、1 〜 3 の英文の（　　）内に当てはまる複合形容詞を選択肢から選び、書き入れましょう。ただし文頭に来る語も小文字で与えられています。

1. The (　　　　　　　　　　) James Webb is named after NASA's administrator during the 1960s.
   長い間（開発が）遅れていたジェームス・ウェッブは、1960 年代の NASA 長官の名前にちなんで命名されている。

2. (　　　　　　　　　　) technical snags bumped the launch nearly a week.
   土壇場の技術的障害により、1 週間近く打ち上げがずれ込んだ。

3. "It's very (　　　　　　　　　　)," said European Space Agency director general Josef Aschbacher.
   「それはとても神経を使うものです」と欧州宇宙機関のジョゼフ・アッシュバッハー長官は述べた。

nerve-racking　　last-minute　　long-delayed

Background Knowledge

⊙ CD 2-18

ジェームス・ウェッブ宇宙望遠鏡について、英文に<u>述べられていないもの</u>を1～4から選びましょう。

　The James Webb Space Telescope's showpiece is a gold-plated mirror more than 21 feet (6.5 meters) across. Protecting the observatory is a wispy, five-layered sunshield, vital for keeping the light-gathering mirror and heat-sensing infrared detectors at subzero temperatures. At 70 feet by 46 feet (21 meters by 14 meters), it's the size of a tennis court.

　If all goes well, the sunshield will be opened three days after liftoff, taking at least five days to unfold and lock into place. Next, the mirror segments should open up like the leaves of a drop-leaf table, 12 days or so into the flight.

The Associated Press

Notes wispy「小さく束ねた」 subzero「氷点下の」 drop-leaf table「垂れ板式テーブル（必要に応じて天板を拡張できる折畳式のテーブル）」

1. 望遠鏡の目玉は、差し渡し 6.5 メートル以上の大きさの金メッキの鏡である。
2. 観測装置を守るのは、5 層構造になった赤外線検出器である。
3. 日除けシールドは、テニスコートほどの大きさである。
4. 順調にいけば、打ち上げの 3 日後には日除けシールドが開かれる。

Newspaper English

地名、人名や団体名など、「その人、そのものだけにつけられた唯一の名前」のことを固有名詞といいます。固有名詞が複数語から成る場合は、語頭を大文字にして表記します。ただし、等位接続詞（and など）や前置詞は、大文字にせず小文字のままで表記されることが多いです。

以下の 1 と 2 の文には固有名詞が含まれています。固有名詞の箇所全てに下線を引きましょう。

1. The National Aeronautics and Space Administration has announced the launch of the James Webb Space Telescope.
   アメリカ航空宇宙局は、ジェームス・ウェッブ宇宙望遠鏡の打ち上げを発表した。

2. Bill Nelson gave a press conference from Florida's Kennedy Space Center.
   ビル・ネルソン氏がフロリダのケネディ宇宙センターから記者会見を行った。

Reading

Space telescope launched on daring quest to behold 1st stars

The world's largest and most powerful space telescope rocketed away Saturday on a high-stakes quest to behold light from the first stars and galaxies and scour the universe for hints of life. NASA's James Webb Space
5   Telescope soared from French Guiana on South America's northeastern coast, riding a European Ariane rocket into the Christmas morning sky. "What an amazing Christmas present," said Thomas Zurbuchen, NASA's science mission chief.

10   The $10 billion observatory hurtled toward its destination 1 million miles (1.6 million kilometers) away, or more than four times beyond the moon. It will take a month to get there and another five months before its infrared eyes are ready to start scanning the cosmos.

15   NASA Administrator Bill Nelson called Webb a time machine that will provide "a better understanding of our universe and our place in it: who we are, what we are, the search that's eternal." "We are going to discover incredible things that we never imagined," Nelson said following
20   liftoff, speaking from Florida's Kennedy Space Center. But he cautioned, "There are still innumerable things that have to work and they have to work perfectly... we know that in great reward there is great risk."

Intended as a successor to the aging Hubble Space
25   Telescope, the long-delayed James Webb is named after NASA's administrator during the 1960s. NASA partnered with the European and Canadian space agencies to build and launch the new 7-ton telescope, with thousands of people from 29 countries working on it since the 1990s.

30   Around the world, astronomers and countless others tuned in, anxious to see Webb finally taking flight after years of setbacks. Last-minute technical snags bumped the launch nearly a week, then gusty wind pushed it to Christmas Day. A few of the launch controllers wore Santa
35   caps in celebration.

launch (...) 「〜を打ち上げる、打ち上げ」
daring 「大胆な」
quest 「探求」

high-stakes 「いちかばちかの」

behold... 「〜を見る」

galaxy 「銀河」

scour... 「〜を捜し回る」

hurtle 「突進していく」

destination 「目的地」

infrared 「赤外線の」

incredible 「驚くべき」

caution... 「〜と警告する」

innumerable 「数え切れない」

reward 「報酬」

tune in 「(テレビ等のチャンネルを) 合わせる」

anxious 「切望して」

setback 「挫折」

gusty wind 「突風」

"We have delivered a Christmas gift today for humanity," said European Space Agency director general Josef Aschbacher. He described it as a special moment, but added, "It's very nerve-racking. I couldn't do launches
40 every single day. This would not be good for my life expectancy."

Cameras on the rocket's upper stage provided one last glimpse of the shimmering telescope against a backdrop of Earth, before it sped away. "That picture will be burned
45 into my mind forever," Zurbuchen told journalists.

The Associated Press

humanity「人類」

life expectancy「寿命」

glimpse「一見、ちらりと見えること」

shimmer「かすかに光る」

backdrop「背景」

speed away「猛スピードで飛び去る」

burn... into ~「…を~に焼き付ける」

● **Comprehension**

本文の内容に合うように、1 の質問の答えとして適当なものを、2 と 3 の英文を完成させるのに適当なものを、a ～ d から選びましょう。

1. How long will it take for the James Webb Telescope to become operational after its launch?

  a. Five months

  b. Six months

  c. One year

  d. Ten years

2. NASA Administrator Bill Nelson

  a. is certain that the telescope will be deployed as planned.

  b. led the space agency during the 1960s.

  c. is cautiously optimistic that the telescope's mission will be a success.

  d. began the Hubble Telescope project in the 1990s.

3. The James Webb Telescope

  a. took off from the Kennedy Space Center in Florida.

  b. will travel approximately 1.6 million miles from Earth.

  c. was built exclusively by NASA.

  d. was launched on Christmas Day.

Summary

🎧 DL 42　◎ CD 2-20

以下の空所 1 ～ 4 に当てはまる語を選択肢から選び、書き入れましょう。

The long-delayed James Webb Space Telescope has been launched, beginning the 1-million-mile (¹·   ) to its destination, where it will observe the earliest stars and search for signs of (²·   ). The project was a collaborative (³·   ) between NASA and the European and Canadian space agencies, as well as thousands of individuals from around the world. Scientists are hopeful that the telescope will provide a deeper (⁴·   ) of the universe.

effort　　journey　　life　　understanding

Insights into Today's World

🎧 DL 43　◎ CD 2-21

以下の対話の空所に、あなたの考えを書いてみましょう。その後、クラスメイトにその内容を伝えてみましょう。

The James Webb Space Telescope's enormous mirror and sunshield are filled with cutting-edge technology.
In the future, in what other areas would you like to see cutting-edge technology applied?

I hope that _____

_____

Chapter 15

A Home for Retired Racehorses

馬たちに第二の人生を

A horse ride at Matsubara Stables (Matsubara Stables)

Key Expressions 1

🎧 DL 44　◎ CD 2-22

音声を聞いて 1 〜 3 の（　　）内に適当な語を書き入れましょう。

1. The operator of the ranch was asked by a horse owner to accept an
   (i _ _ _ _ _ _) thoroughbred that could no longer race.
   その牧場主は、もうレースに出られない負傷したサラブレッドを受け入れてほしいと、ある馬主から頼まれた。

2. A racehorse (t _ _ _ _ _ _) held charity events to raise funds for caring for
   retired horses.
   ある競走馬の調教師が、引退した馬たちの世話のための寄付を求めて、チャリティーイベントを行った。

3. There are no riding sessions once the (t _ _ _ _ _ _ _ _ _ _) outside gets hotter
   than 30 degrees.
   外の気温が 30℃ を超えると乗馬体験は行われない。

Key Expressions 2

-ic は名詞を形容詞にする接尾辞で、「〜の、〜の性質を持つ、〜的な」といった意味を持ちます。

枠内の接尾辞の説明と日本語訳を参考に、1〜5の名詞を形容詞にして〔　　〕内に書き入れましょう。

1. cube（立方体）　　　→〔　　　　　　　　　　　　　〕（立方体の）
2. alcohol（アルコール）→〔　　　　　　　　　　　　　〕（アルコール性の、
　　　　　　　　　　　　　　　　　　　　　　　　　　　　　　アルコール中毒の）
3. economy（経済）　　　→〔　　　　　　　　　　　　　〕（経済の）
4. tragedy（悲劇）　　　→〔　　　　　　　　　　　　　〕（悲劇的な）
5. symbol（象徴）　　　→〔　　　　　　　　　　　　　〕（象徴的な）

Key Expressions 3

不定詞の副詞的用法は、「〜するために」（目的）、「〜した結果…になる」（結果）、「〜して」（感情の原因）などの意味を表します。下線部に含まれる不定詞の用法がどの意味に該当するかに注意しながら、1〜3の英文の日本語訳を完成させましょう。

1. Masafumi Matsubara <u>was shocked to learn</u> that many racehorses are put down after retirement.

   松原正文氏は、多くの競走馬が引退後に安楽死させられる ＿＿＿＿＿＿＿＿＿＿＿＿＿＿＿。

2. Akeboshi has been working with Matsubara <u>to protect horses who would be culled</u> because of their wounds or poor performance.

   明星氏は、けがや成績不振のために ＿＿＿＿＿＿＿＿＿＿＿＿＿＿＿＿＿
   松原氏とともに取り組んできた。

   Note cull...「〜を処分する、淘汰する」

3. Akeboshi believes that children will <u>grow up to make changes</u> if they understand the difficulties that horses face.

   子どもたちが馬の直面する困難を理解すれば、＿＿＿＿＿＿＿＿＿＿＿＿＿＿＿
   と明星氏は信じている。

Background Knowledge

CD 2-23

松原ステーブルスという牧場が 2021 年に始めた来場者向けのプロジェクトの内容について、英文に<u>述べられていないもの</u>を 1 〜 4 から選びましょう。

In 2021, Matsubara Stables started a project where visitors can live close to horses on a vacant rental home near the farm. Those who want to build careers related to horses can use the opportunity to learn how to keep and handle the animals alongside the facility's staffers. The ranch is likewise equipped with a camping site, and a group of campers can set up their tents there for 2,000 yen per night.

The Asahi Shimbun Asia & Japan Watch

Note staffer「職員、スタッフ」

1. 農場近くの空き家を借りて馬の近くに暮らすことができる。
2. 馬に関わる仕事に就きたい人は、馬の扱い方などを学ぶことができる。
3. 施設のスタッフの仕事を手伝うことで、1 日 2,000 円ほどの収入が得られる。
4. 農場にはキャンプ場もあり、グループでそこにテントを張ることができる。

Newspaper English

as... as 〜の同等比較表現の…の部分に much, many, little などの語を入れて、「〜も（たくさん）」または「〜しか、たった〜」という意味を表すことができます。数量の多さや少なさを強調する働きがあります。

日本語訳を参考に、1 〜 3 の英文の（　　）内に当てはまる語を選択肢から選び、書き入れましょう。

1. In Japan, as (   ) as 7,000 horses are euthanized each year.
   日本では毎年 7,000 頭もの馬が安楽死させられる。

2. With a reservation made a day in advance, a visitor can try out a horse ride for as (   ) as 500 yen.
   前日までに予約すれば、来場者はたった 500 円で乗馬を体験をすることができる。

3. Thoroughbred horses are quite expensive, and their upkeep can be as (   ) as $60,000 a year.
   サラブレッドはかなり高額で、その飼育費は年間 6 万ドルにもなる可能性がある。

much　　many　　little

Reading

Niigata farm rescues retired racehorses from sad homestretch

As a young jockey, Masafumi Matsubara was astonished to learn that many racehorses are put down after retirement since there are few places in Japan where they can spend their golden years.

5 "If racehorses win competitions, their jockeys and trainers will gain honor and those who bet on them will win money," said Matsubara. "Horses are living creatures that provide dreams for people but they are treated like disposable objects."

10 In Japan, as many as 7,000 horses are euthanized each year. Matsubara set out on his mission 16 years ago to change the tragic fate of those animals. He established a stock farm in Tainai, Niigata Prefecture that accepts horses that would otherwise be put down so that they 15 could live out their lives.

The ranch, named Matsubara Stables, currently keeps 16 retired horses. Many are thoroughbreds that can no longer race due to injuries, but their ranks also include a miniature horse, a breed indigenous to Japan, and a few 20 other species.

Matsubara hails from Hidaka, a famous horse-producing area in Hokkaido. His father worked there transporting trees cut down from the mountains using horses born in the nation's northernmost prefecture. Matsubara has been 25 close to horses since childhood, so the animals are "as important as people" to him.

He was invited to become a jockey at age 16 by a horsebreaker working for a racecourse in Niigata Prefecture who visited his father's stock farm. After 30 Matsubara retired from his career in horseracing, he served as a stable lad and a trainer, and then opened his own farm in the hopes of saving as many horses as possible. He took care of his horses day and night when they fell ill. He attended to 15 of these horses in their final 35 hours.

homestretch「ゴール前の直線コース、終局」
astonished「驚いた、びっくりした」

golden years「老後」
competition「レース、競技会」
gain honor「名誉を得る」
bet「(金などを) 賭ける」

disposable「使い捨ての」

set out on...「～を始める」
fate「運命」
stock farm「牧場」

live out one's life「余生を送る」

rank「部類、種類」
miniature horse「ミニチュアホース」
a breed indigenous to Japan「日本の在来種」
hail from...「～の出身である」
horse-producing area「馬の産地」
northernmost「最北の」

horsebreaker「調馬師 (馬をさまざまな仕事で使えるよう訓練する人)」
racecourse「競馬場」
serve as...「～として働く」
stable lad「厩務員 (調教師の指示に従って担当馬の世話をする係)」

Yasutaka Akeboshi, who worked with Matsubara, has now taken over operation of Matsubara Stables. In April 2021, it became a nonprofit organization with Akeboshi as its head.

40　Matsubara Stables provides educational activities on its grounds and sometimes visits the local kindergartens with the horses. Akeboshi believes that children will grow up to make changes if they understand the difficulties that horses face.

The Asahi Shimbun Asia & Japan Watch

45

day and night「四六時中、昼夜を問わず」

take over...「〜を引き継ぐ」

nonprofit organization「非営利団体［組織］、NPO 法人」

educational activity「教育的アクティビティ」

kindergarten「幼稚園」

Comprehension

本文の内容に合うように、1 と 3 の質問の答えとして適当なものを、2 の英文を完成させるのに適当なものを、a 〜 d から選びましょう。

1. Why are so many racehorses in Japan put down after their racing days are over?
    a. They have not won enough racing competitions.
    b. Disposing of the horses is considered an honorable practice.
    c. Only specific types of horses can be cared for beyond retirement.
    d. There are not enough facilities to care for them.

2. Matsubara Stables
    a. currently houses 16 retired thoroughbred horses.
    b. is located in the area where Matsubara grew up.
    c. welcomes visitors to the property for educational purposes.
    d. primarily cares for horses of breeds indigenous to Japan.

3. Which of the following positions has Matsubara NOT held?
    a. Stable lad
    b. A director of a nonprofit organization
    c. Jockey
    d. Trainer

Summary

🎧 DL 45 💿 CD 2-25

以下の空所1〜4に当てはまる語を選択肢から選び、書き入れましょう。

Masafumi Matsubara, a former jockey, has established a ranch that serves as a safe (¹.   ) for horses that would otherwise be put down, including retired or injured racehorses. Inspired by a lifelong (².   ) for horses, he wanted to provide a space where they could be treated with dignity and avoid the grim (³.   ) of so many other horses in Japan. The ranch also provides an educational (⁴.   ) for children, with the purpose of inspiring sympathy for the animals.

haven   fate   respect   experience

Insights into Today's World

🎧 DL 46 💿 CD 2-26

以下の対話の空所に、あなたのアイデアを書いてみましょう。その後、クラスメイトにその内容を伝えてみましょう。

There are few safe places for retired horses, since running that kind of facility entails much labor but yields little profit.
Is there anything we can do to help them?

I recommend that _____

_____

Chapter 16

Distant Memory Leads a Man to Home

手書きの地図で家族と再会

City of Zhaotong, Yunnan province (©Day Ice | Dreamstime.com)

Key Expressions 1

🎧 DL 47   ◎ CD 2-27

音声を聞いて 1 〜 3 の（　　）内に適当な語を書き入れましょう。

1. Li was only 4 years old when he was taken away from his (n _ _ _ _ _) village in Yunnan province.

   李氏が雲南省の彼が生まれた村から連れ去られたとき、彼はたった 4 歳だった。

2. "I recognized my mother at a (g _ _ _ _ _)," Li said.

   「私はひと目で母だとわかりました」と李氏は述べた。

3. As Li walked toward his family, he (c _ _ _ _ _ _ _ _) on the ground in emotion.

   李氏は家族のほうに歩み寄ると、感極まって地面にくずれ落ちた。

Key Expressions 2

接頭辞 re- は、主に「再び、繰り返し」という意味を、元になる語に付け加えます。
例：build「〜を建てる」→ rebuild「〜を再建する、建て直す」

枠内の説明を参考に、以下の 1 〜 5 の日本語の意味になるように、選択肢の動詞に re- を付け加えて (　　) 内に書き入れましょう。

1. 再び描く　　　（　　　　　　　　　　　　　　　　　）
2. 再接続する　　（　　　　　　　　　　　　　　　　　）
3. 再確認する　　（　　　　　　　　　　　　　　　　　）
4. 再発見する　　（　　　　　　　　　　　　　　　　　）
5. 再会する　　　（　　　　　　　　　　　　　　　　　）

connect　　unite　　confirm　　draw　　discover

Key Expressions 3

日本語訳を参考に、1 〜 3 の英文の（　　）内に当てはまる語句を選択肢から選び、書き入れましょう。ただし文頭に来る語も小文字で与えられています。

1. The abducted boy asked the man to take him home (

　　　　　　　　　　　).

  誘拐された男の子は、その男に家に連れて帰ってほしいと何度も何度も頼んだ。

2. It took Li only 10 minutes to draw what he had drawn (

　　　　　　　　　　　) times as a child.

  子どものころ何千回と描いたものを描くのに、李氏は 10 分しかかからなかった。

3. (

　　　　　　　　　　　　　　　　　　　　　　　) passed by that he

  didn't think about his real family.

  本当の家族のことを考えない日は一日もなかった。

not a day　　over and over again　　thousands of

Background Knowledge

CD 2-28

中国の児童誘拐の現状について、英文に述べられているものを 1 〜 4 から選びましょう。

　Li was inspired to look for his biological family after two reunions made headlines last year. In July, a Chinese father, Guo Gangtang, was united with his son after searching for 24 years, and in December, Sun Haiyang was reunited with his kidnapped son after 14 years.

　Reports of child abductions occur regularly in China, though how often they happen is unclear. The problem is aggravated by restrictions that until 2015 allowed most urban couples only one child.

The Associated Press

Notes be inspired to... 「〜する気になる」 biological 「生物学的な、血のつながった」 make a headline 「トップニュースになる」 aggravate... 「〜を悪化させる」

1. 誘拐された娘を 24 年間かけて探し出した父親のことがニュースになった。
2. 14 年前に誘拐された息子の情報提供を呼びかける父親のことが話題になった。
3. 中国で子どもの誘拐がどのくらい頻繁に起こっているかは、よくわかっていない。
4. 2015 年までは、都会に住む夫婦だけが子どもを 1 人持つことができた。

Newspaper English

 英語は語順が比較的厳密な言語ですが、主語と述語動詞の順序が入れ替わることがあり、これを倒置といいます。疑問文など文法的な倒置のほかに、強調のための倒置があります。強調される部分が文頭に置かれ、多くの場合主語と述語動詞が倒置されます。

日本語訳を参考に 1 〜 3 の英文の〔　　〕内の語句を正しい語順に並べ替えましょう。

1. Not until he was 32, [to find / did / try / he] his biological family.
   32 歳になるまで、彼は血のつながっている家族を探そうとはしなかった。

   _____

2. Etched in his memory [of his village / was / the landscape].
   記憶に焼きついていたのは、彼の村の風景だった。

   _____

3. Lucky [son / the mother / is / whose] has a good memory.
   記憶力のよい息子を持つ母は幸せである。

   _____

Reading

Map helps Chinese man reunite with his family after decades

Li Jingwei was a victim of child trafficking. In 1989 when he was 4 years old, a neighbor lured him away by saying they would go look at cars, which were rare in rural villages.

5　That was the last time he saw his home. He remembers being taken on a train. Eventually he was sold to a family in another province.

"Because I was too young, only 4, and I hadn't gone to school yet, I couldn't remember anything, including the
10　names" of his parents and hometown, he said. Etched in his memory, however, was the landscape of his village.

Li said he drew maps of his village every day until he was 13 so that he wouldn't forget. Before he reached school age, he would draw them on the ground, and after
15　entering school he drew them in notebooks.

More than 30 years after his abduction, Li decided to look for his biological family. He spoke with his adoptive parents for clues and consulted DNA databases, but nothing turned up. Then he found volunteers who
20　suggested he post a video of himself on Douyin, a social media platform, along with the map he drew from memory. It took him only 10 minutes to redraw what he had drawn hundreds, perhaps thousands of times as a child, he said.

25　That post received tens of thousands of views. By then, Li said the police had already narrowed down locations based on his DNA sample, and his hand-drawn map helped villagers identify a family.

Li finally connected with his mother over the telephone.
30　She asked about a scar on his chin which she said was caused by a fall from a ladder. "When she mentioned the scar, I knew it was her," Li said.

Other details and recollections fell into place, and a DNA test confirmed his heritage. In an emotional reunion
35　on New Year's Day, he saw his mother for the first time

decade「10 年」

victim「被害者」
child trafficking「児童（人身）売買」
lure... away「〜をおびき出す」
rural「田舎の」
eventually「最終的に」
province「省、州、県など」

adoptive parents「養父母」
clue「手がかり」
consult...「〜を調べる」
turn up「見つかる」
Douyin「抖音（中国版 TikTok のこと）」
along with...「〜と一緒に」

narrow down...「（範囲など）を絞り込む」
identify...「〜を特定する」
connect with...「〜と連絡をとる」
scar「傷痕」
ladder「梯子」
mention...「〜のことを口にする」
detail「詳細」
recollection「思い出」

since he was four.

　　As Li walked toward her, he collapsed on the ground in emotion. Lifted up by his younger brother and sister, he finally hugged his mother.

The Associated Press

fall into place「つじつまが合う」

confirm...「～を確認する、裏付ける」

heritage「遺産（ここでは「遺伝的な遺産、血統」の意)」

emotional「感動的な」

Comprehension

本文の内容に合うように、1と3の英文を完成させるのに適当なものを、2の質問の答えとして適当なものを、a〜dから選びましょう。

1. Li Jingwei could not remember the names of his parents or hometown because

　　a. he became confused on the train ride to another province.

　　b. the trauma of being abducted affected his memory.

　　c. his adoptive parents refused to let him go to school.

　　d. he was not yet old enough to memorize such information.

2. Which of the following is NOT a tactic that Li Jingwei used to find his biological family as an adult?

　　a. He searched for them in various DNA databases.

　　b. He repeatedly drew a map of his village in notebooks and on the ground.

　　c. He assessed whether the couple who adopted him could provide any information.

　　d. He consulted with the police.

3. Li Jingwei's mother asked him about a scar on his chin

　　a. because she was concerned about the extent of the injury.

　　b. as confirmation that he was in fact her son.

　　c. because the map he drew was not accurate enough.

　　d. to apologize for allowing him to fall from a ladder.

Summary

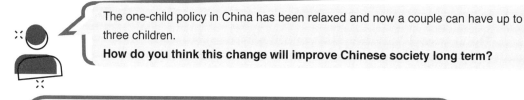

DL 48　CD 2-30

以下の空所 1 〜 4 に当てはまる語を選択肢から選び、書き入れましょう。

Li Jingwei, a Chinese man who was abducted at age four, was finally reunited with his (1.   ) family after more than 30 years. While he could not remember (2.   ) details about his family and hometown, he managed to retain a (3.   ) map of his village that he repeatedly drew throughout his childhood. By sharing it on social media, the map played a (4.   ) role in the process of finally tracking down his family.

vital　　specific　　biological　　mental

Insights into Today's World

DL 49　CD 2-31

以下の対話の空所に、あなたの考えを書いてみましょう。その後、クラスメイトにその内容を伝えてみましょう。

The one-child policy in China has been relaxed and now a couple can have up to three children.
How do you think this change will improve Chinese society long term?

To be honest, _____

_____

Chapter 17

Asian Americans Making their Presence Known

アジア系アメリカ人にとっての新たな歴史

Sokhary Chau, Mayor of Lowell, MA (AP/Aflo)

● Key Expressions 1

🎧 DL 50   ◎ CD 2-32

音声を聞いて 1 ～ 3 の （　　）内に適当な語を書き入れましょう。

1. Sokhary Chau was elected as the first Cambodian American (m _ _ _ _) in the United States.

ソカリー・チャウ氏が、アメリカ初のカンボジア系アメリカ人の市長に選出された。

2. In 1981, Chau arrived in Pennsylvania as a (r _ _ _ _ _ _) sponsored by the Catholic Church.

チャウ氏は 1981 年に、カトリック教会の支援で難民としてペンシルベニア州に到着した。

3. Chau says that the United States is a country where (d _ _ _ _ _ _ _ _) is possible.

チャウ氏は、アメリカは民主主義が可能な国だと語っている。

Key Expressions 2

ある一つの単語の語形が変化してできた単語のことを「派生語」と呼びます。品詞の異なる派生語をまとめて覚えておくと、効率的に語彙を増やすことができます。

1 ～ 5 の名詞の日本語訳を a ～ e から選び、[　　] 内に書き入れましょう。また、それぞれの名詞の元になった動詞の原形を（　　）内に書き入れましょう。

1. survival 　　 [　] 　　　 ← (　　　　　　　　　　)
2. execution 　 [　] 　　　 ← (　　　　　　　　　　)
3. immigration [　] 　　　 ← (　　　　　　　　　　)
4. swearing 　 [　] 　　　 ← (　　　　　　　　　　)
5. election 　　 [　] 　　　 ← (　　　　　　　　　　)

　　　　 a. 処刑 　　　 b. 宣誓 　　　 c. 移住 　　　 d. 生き延びること 　　　 e. 当選、選挙

Key Expressions 3

大きな数を英語で読む場合のルールとして、以下を覚えておきましょう。

- **桁の大きな数**：「下 3 桁ごと」にコンマで区切り、3 桁のところで thousand、6 桁のところで million と単位を付けます。→ 1 0 0,0 0 0,0 0 0

    million thousand

- **西暦**：前半と後半の 2 桁ずつに分けて読みます。「2010 年以降」の西暦については、thousand を使って読むパターンもあります。また、2000 年～ 2009 年では two thousand nine のように thousand を使うことが一般的です。

1 と 2 の下線部の数字の読み方を、例のようにつづりで書きましょう。

例：Sokhary Chau is 49 years old. 　　　 (forty-nine)

1. There are more than 115,000 residents in the city.

   (　　　　　　　　　　　　　　　　　)

2. The swearing-in ceremony was held on January 3rd, 2022.

   2 桁ずつ区切って読むパターン：

   (　　　　　　　　　　　　　　　　　)

   thousand を使って読むパターン：

   (　　　　　　　　　　　　　　　　　)

Background Knowledge

CD 2-33

アメリカ初のカンボジア系アメリカ人市長となったソカリー・チャウ氏と彼の家族の経歴について、英文に述べられていないものを1〜4から選びましょう。

In an interview, Sokhary Chau said he was around nine years old when his family initially settled in Pittsburgh, Pennsylvania, with the help of the Catholic Church, which was an experience that prompted the family to convert to Christianity. They made their way to Lowell's growing Cambodian community in the mid-1980s, where some of his older siblings immediately set to work in local factories.

Chau, however, continued his studies and eventually earned a scholarship to Phillips Academy, an exclusive boarding school in nearby Andover. He went on to Macalester College in St. Paul, Minnesota, where he studied economics and political science, also on a scholarship.

The Associated Press

1. ペンシルベニア州のピッツバーグに移住したとき、チャウ氏は9歳くらいであった。
2. チャウ氏一家は元々カトリック教徒であったことから、アメリカに移住する際に教会からの支援を受けることができた。
3. チャウ氏のきょうだいの中には、ローウェル市の工場で働き始めた者もいた。
4. チャウ氏は、ミネソタ州のマカレスター大学で、経済学と政治学を学んだ。

Newspaper English

英文記事のヘッドライン（見出し）には、通常の英語とは異なる文法のルールがあります。時制もその一つです。過去の出来事は「現在形」で表し、未来の出来事は「to + 動詞の原形」で表されることが多くあります。

1と2のヘッドラインの（　　）内に当てはまる動詞を選択肢から選び、適当な形に変化させて書き入れましょう。

1. Nation's 1st Cambodian American mayor (　　　　　　　　　　) office
   国内で初めてのカンボジア系アメリカ人市長、就任

2. Sokhary Chau (　　　　　　　　　) as mayor for next two years in Lowell
   ソカリー・チャウ氏、今後2年間ローウェル市で市長を務める

serve   take

Reading

1st Cambodian American mayor in U.S. takes office

A refugee who survived the Khmer Rouge's brutal rule has become the first Cambodian American mayor in the United States. Chau's election follows the ascendance of new Boston Mayor Michelle Wu, whose parents
5 immigrated to the U.S. from Taiwan. She was sworn in last November as Boston's first woman and first person of color elected to the post.

Sokhary Chau, a city councilor in Lowell, Massachusetts, was unanimously picked by his council
10 peers to assume the legislative body's top post on Monday. He also became the city's first Asian American mayor. "God bless America, right? I was a refugee, now I'm mayor of a major city in Massachusetts," the 49-year-old, who works for the U.S. Social Security Administration, said
15 after being officially sworn in.

Chau, in his inaugural remarks, reflected on his family's perilous escape from Cambodia and the former industrial city of Lowell's deep immigrant roots.

Located on the Merrimack River near the New
20 Hampshire state line, Lowell was an early center of America's textile industry, drawing waves of European and Latin American immigrants over generations. Today, the city of more than 115,000 residents is nearly 25% Asian and home to the nation's second-largest Cambodian
25 community.

"As a proud Cambodian American, I am standing on the shoulders of many immigrants who came before me to build this city," Chau said Monday before a crowd that included his wife and two teenage sons.
30 Chau recounted how his father, a captain in the Cambodian army, was executed by the communist Khmer Rouge in 1975 during the country's civil war. He said his mother, who died last year, managed to keep her seven children alive for four years, surviving "land mines,
35 jungles, hunger, sickness and uncertainty" to deliver them

brutal「残虐な」

ascendance「当選、優勢」

be sworn in「就任の宣誓をする」

post「役職」

councilor「議員」
unanimously「全会一致で」
peer「同僚」
assume...「～に就任する」
legislative body「議会、立法機関」
bless...「～を祝福する」

inaugural「就任の」
reflect on...「～を振り返る」
perilous「危険な」
industrial「工業の」

textile「繊維の」
draw...「～を引き寄せる」
immigrant「移民」
resident「居住者」

proud「誇り高い」

recount...「～を詳しく語る」
army「陸軍」
communist「共産主義の」

land mine「地雷」
hunger「飢え」

safely to the U.S.

    Chau said America may not have "streets paved with gold" as his family imagined while living in refugee camps, but it's a land where democracy is possible because of

40 "systems of checks and balances" and principles like fairness, equality and transparency.

    "We can no longer be just victims," he said as he closed his inaugural remarks. "It is our time now to be leaders and to succeed."

45   *The Associated Press*

| uncertainty「不安」 |
| pave...「〜を舗装する」 |
| checks and balances「抑制と均衡」 |
| principle「原則」 |
| fairness「公平」 |
| equality「平等」 |
| transparency「透明性」 |
| no longer...「もはや〜でない」 |
| victim「犠牲者」 |

参考
・Khmer Rouge (l. 1)「クメール・ルージュ」：カンボジアの反政府組織。1970年代、反対派を虐殺する極端な共産主義革命を行った。
・checks and balances (l. 40)「抑制と均衡」：権力が特定の分野に偏るのを防ぐため、立法・司法・行政の各分野が互いに権力を抑制・監視し合うシステムのこと。

Comprehension

本文の内容に合うように、1と2の英文を完成させるのに適当なものを、3の質問の答えとして適当なものを、a〜dから選びましょう。

1. In his inaugural remarks, Sokhary Chau did NOT comment on
    a. his work at the U.S. Social Security Administration.
    b. the death of his father.
    c. the role that immigrants played in the city's history.
    d. the dangers his family overcame to escape Cambodia.

2. The city of Lowell
    a. has the largest Cambodian population in the U.S.
    b. is historically associated with the American textile industry.
    c. maintains a population of 1.15 million people.
    d. is located in the state of New Hampshire.

3. Which of the following is true about Sokhary Chau?
    a. His mother died in 1979, four years after his father was executed.
    b. He has seven siblings, all of whom escaped to the U.S.
    c. He is married and has two sons in their twenties.
    d. He believes in the potential of U.S. democracy.

Summary

以下の空所 1 ～ 4 に当てはまる語を選択肢から選び、書き入れましょう。

Following recent electoral success by Asian Americans, Sokhary Chau, a Cambodian American who (1.　　　　　　　　) the horrors of the Khmer Rouge in the 1970s, was (2.　　　　　　　) mayor of Lowell, Massachusetts. This marks the first time a Cambodian American will serve as mayor of a U.S. city. Upon taking office, Chau (3.　　　　　　) his family story, acknowledged immigrants who came before him, and (4.　　　　　) the U.S. system of government.

> elected　shared　survived　praised

Insights into Today's World

🎧 DL 52　◎ CD 2-36

以下の対話の空所に、あなたの意見を書いてみましょう。その後、クラスメイトにその内容を伝えてみましょう。

Massachusetts has appointed the United States' first Cambodian American mayor. Along with the United States, Japan is also increasingly racially and ethnically diverse.
What do you think are the benefits of promoting diversity in society?

I believe that _____

_____

Chapter 18

Rising Conductor Faces the Music

新世代の指揮者

Nodoka Okisawa (© Felix Broede)

Key Expressions 1

🎧 DL 53   ◎ CD 2-37

音声を聞いて1〜3の（　　）内に適当な語を書き入れましょう。

1. The audience (a _ _ _ _ _ _ _ _) as Okisawa finished conducting Sibelius' Symphony No. 2.

   沖澤氏がシベリウスの交響曲第2番を指揮し終えたとき、観客は拍手喝采した。

2. Okisawa was an assistant to Kirill Petrenko, the Chief (C _ _ _ _ _ _ _ _) of the Berlin Philharmonic.

   沖澤氏は、ベルリン・フィルハーモニー管弦楽団の首席指揮者キリル・ペトレンコ氏のアシスタントであった。

3. The city of Kyoto Symphony Orchestra has (a _ _ _ _ _ _ _ _) Nodoka Okisawa as its new Chief Conductor, starting from April 2023.

   京都市交響楽団は、2023年4月から新しい常任指揮者として沖澤のどか氏を任命した。

Key Expressions 2

英語にはラテン語やギリシャ語からの外来語が少なくありません。こうした語はラテン語やギリシャ語特有の語尾変化で複数形を表すため、注意が必要です。ただし、こうした語も英語として定着すると、語尾に -(e)s をつけて複数形を表す場合があります。

日本語の意味を参考に、以下の表の 1 ～ 5 の空所に適当な語を書き入れましょう。

	単数形	複数形	日本語の意味
1	_____	data	データ
2	podium	podiums, _____	指揮台、表彰台、演壇
3	phenomenon	phenomenons, _____	現象、事象
4	index	indexes, _____	指標、指数
5	_____	media	媒体、伝達手段

Key Expressions 3

英語では共通する語句の重複を避けるため、省いても意味上混乱を招かない場合、2 度目は省略するのが一般的です。

例：My sisters play the piano, and I play the violin.
　　→ My sisters play the piano, and I the violin.

日本語訳を参考に、1 ～ 3 の英文で省略できる部分に下線を引き、その下線部を除いた形で英文を音読してみましょう。

1. Okisawa's father is a public servant, and her mother is a homemaker.
   沖澤氏の父親は公務員、母親は専業主婦である。

2. The student decided to major in music, and her cousin decided to major in linguistics.
   その学生は音楽を専攻する決心をし、彼女のいとこは言語学を専攻する決心をした。

3. At the final round of the competition, the pianist played Chopin's Piano Concerto No.2, and her friend played Chopin's Piano Concerto No.1.
   そのコンクールのファイナルで、そのピアニストはショパンのピアノ協奏曲第 2 番を演奏し、彼女の友人は第 1 番を演奏した。

● Background Knowledge

 CD 2-38

クラシック音楽界の実情について、英文に<u>述べられていないもの</u>を 1 ～ 4 から選びましょう。

　In the classical music world, which is said to be dominated by men, a paradoxical phenomenon of a boom in female conductors has been seen.

　Under such circumstances, Okisawa noticed that there is a divide between male and female conductors. "I've been told, 'Women are given unfair advantages,'" Okisawa said. "Eliminating that [perception] would be good."

The Japan News

Notes　paradoxical phenomenon「矛盾する現象」　eliminate...「～をなくす、除去する」

1. 男性優位と言われるなかで女性指揮者の躍進が見られる。

2. 沖澤氏は、男性指揮者と女性指揮者の間に隔たりがあることに気づいた。

3. 沖澤氏は「女性が不当な優位性を与えられている」と言われたことがある。

4. 女性指揮者のほうが優位である状況になることを沖澤氏は願っている。

● Newspaper English

 英文記事では、名詞から派生した動詞がしばしば用いられます。以下の例では「～を解雇する」の意味で ax（名詞の意味は「斧」）が使われています。
例：The company is going to ax 50 employees this fall.
名詞「斧」のもつイメージが動詞の意味にも反映して、鮮明な印象を与える効果があります。

日本語訳を参考に、1 と 2 の英文の（　　）内に入る語を選択肢から選び、必要であれば形を変えて書き入れましょう。

1. When she was a high school student, Okisawa was only (　　　　　　　　　) universities reputed to have good student orchestras.
高校生だったころ、沖澤氏は学生オーケストラの評判が良い大学ばかりに注目していた。

2. The members of the orchestra are expected to (　　　　　　　　) their opinions freely.
そのオーケストラのメンバーは、自由に意見を述べることが期待されている。

voice　　　eye

Reading

Rising conductor Nodoka Okisawa faces music naturally

With a baton in her hand and wins in major classical music competitions under her belt, Nodoka Okisawa is a flourishing up-and-coming conductor living in Berlin.

Born in 1987 in Aomori Prefecture, Okisawa earned
5 bachelor's and master's degrees at Tokyo University of the Arts as well as a master's degree at the Hanns Eisler School of Music in Berlin. In 2018, she became the first woman to win the Tokyo International Music Competition for Conducting. She also won the grand prix at the
10 Besancon International Competition for Young Conductors in France in 2019.

Okisawa's father is a public servant, and her mother a homemaker. She took cello and piano lessons as a child and played the oboe in her high school brass band. She
15 decided to become a conductor in the winter of her second year in high school. Okisawa originally wanted to study linguistics in college, but then realized she was only eyeing universities reputed to have good student orchestras. So, she decided to major in music. "I thought it
20 wasn't too late to enter the department of conducting, unlike the department of instrumental music," she said. "I was so naive."

Okisawa somehow mastered the music for the entrance exam enough to pass it. But difficult days awaited her.
25 Since the other students were much more advanced, she was tormented by an inferiority complex. She even had trouble climbing the conductor's podium. Okisawa became mentally and physically exhausted, and returned to her parents' home for six months.

30 After finishing graduate school, she studied in Germany. The experience led to a major turning point. "I began to think I might fit in," Okisawa said upon seeing the diverse group of people in the music world. "I realized that I didn't necessarily have to be successful."

35 When asked about her vision for the future, she said she

under one's belt「(経験を）積んで、身につけて」
flourish「活躍する、頭角を現す」
up-and-coming 「勢いのある」
bachelor's degree「学士号」
master's degree「修士号」
Tokyo University of the Arts「東京芸術大学」

department of conducting「指揮科」
instrumental music「器楽」
naive「考えが甘い」
await...「〜を待つ、待ち受ける」
advanced「進んだ、上級の」
torment...「〜をひどく苦しめる」
inferiority complex「劣等感コンプレックス」
mentally and physically exhausted「心身共に疲れ果て」
graduate school「大学院」
fit in「(環境などに）溶け込む、なじむ」
diverse「多様な」

would like to work in theater. "Taking into account my personality, I can't imagine myself flying around the world conducting top-notch orchestras one after another. I want to narrow down the number of my engagements and
40 concentrate on them. I hope to work in the opera world for a while."

The Japan News

take into account... 「～を考慮する」
top-notch 「一流の」
narrow down... 「～を絞る」
engagement 「仕事」

参考
・Hanns Eisler School of Music in Berlin (l. 6)「ハンス・アイスラー音楽大学ベルリン」：1950 年設立の音楽大学。世界最高峰の講師陣による指導に定評がある。
・the Tokyo International Music Competition for Conducting (l. 8)「東京国際音楽コンクール〈指揮〉」：1966 年創設の、若手指揮者の登竜門とされるコンクール。
・the Besancon International Music Competition for Young Conductors (l. 9)「ブザンソン国際若手指揮者コンクール」：1951 年創設の、世界的に知られる指揮コンクール。日本人の優勝者は 1959 年の小澤征爾氏から沖澤のどか氏まで計 10 人。

Comprehension

本文の内容に合うように、1 と 3 の英文を完成させるのに適当なものを、2 の質問の答えとして適当なものを、a～d から選びましょう。

1. Nodoka Okisawa
   a. studied both music and linguistics in college.
   b. was born to a family of musicians.
   c. won the second in the Besancon International Competition for Young Conductors.
   d. has earned multiple master's degrees.

2. Which of the statements about Okisawa's high school days is NOT true?
   a. She belonged to the brass band.
   b. She decided to specialize in conducting.
   c. She started taking cello lessons.
   d. She thought it was too late to enter the department of instrumental music.

3. Okisawa says she can't imagine herself conducting world-class orchestras throughout the world because

  a. she is still suffering from an inferiority complex.

  b. she prefers to stay in one location.

  c. such a lifestyle does not fit her temperament.

  d. she prefers the diversity of the people in the theater world.

● Summary  DL 54 CD 2-40

以下の空所 1 ～ 4 に当てはまる語を選択肢から選び、書き入れましょう。

The winner of multiple (¹·   ), world renowned Japanese conductor, Nodoka Okisawa has won (²·   ) for her abilities, both in Japan and abroad. Despite the self-doubt she felt in her early days, she has found her (³·   ) in the music world and has managed to thrive. She currently resides in Berlin and hopes for an (⁴·   ) to conduct opera in the future.

place   competitions   opportunity   acclaim

● Insights into Today's World  DL 55 CD 2-41

以下の対話の空所に、あなたのアイデアを書いてみましょう。その後、クラスメイトにその内容を伝えてみましょう。

Okisawa suffered from an inferiority complex after she entered Tokyo University of the Arts. But actually I believe everybody has some kind of inferiority complex. **Do you have any ideas about how to manage one?**

That's a difficult question, but _____

_____

Chapter 19

Roadmap to a Zero-Emissions Society

原発は盾か矛か

A nuclear power plant on the Rhone River in France (© Adeliepenguin | Dreamstime.com)

Key Expressions 1

🎧 DL 56   ◎ CD 2-42

音声を聞いて 1 ～ 3 の（　　）内に適当な語を書き入れましょう。

1. (S _ _ _ _) rises from cooling towers of a nuclear power plant on the Rhone River in France.

   水蒸気が、フランスのローヌ川沿いにある原子力発電所の冷却塔から立ちのぼっている。

2. Nuclear power produces very low CO_2 emissions, but its radioactive waste disposal can have a (s _ _ _ _ _ _ _ _ _) impact on the environment.

   原子力発電は、二酸化炭素の排出量が非常に少ない反面、放射性廃棄物の処理で環境に重大な影響を与える可能性がある。

3. Natural gas emits roughly half the CO_2 emissions of coal when burned in power plants, but gas infrastructure is (a _ _ _ _ _ _ _ _ _) with leaks of methane, a potent planet-warming gas.

   天然ガスは発電所で燃やすとき石炭の約半分の二酸化炭素を排出するが、ガスインフラは、強力な地球温暖化ガスであるメタンの漏れに関連がある。

Key Expressions 2

動詞の語尾に -able や -ible という接尾辞を付加すると、「〜できる、〜しうる」という意味を表す形容詞になります。

以下の 1 〜 5 は、エネルギー問題を扱う文脈で頻出する動詞です。（　　）内に -able あるいは -ible を付加した形容詞を書き入れ、［　　］内にその意味を選択肢から選んで書き入れましょう。

1. sustain　→（　　　　　　　）［　　　　　　　　］
2. renew　→（　　　　　　　）［　　　　　　　　］
3. convert　→（　　　　　　　）［　　　　　　　　］
4. burn　→（　　　　　　　）［　　　　　　　　］
5. dispose　→（　　　　　　　）［　　　　　　　　］

処理できる、使い捨ての　　　持続可能な　　　再生可能な　　　可燃の　　　転換できる

Key Expressions 3

日本語訳を参考に、1 〜 3 の英文の（　　）内に当てはまる前置詞を選択肢から選び、書き入れましょう。

1. There is a role for natural gas and nuclear power (　　　　　) a means to facilitate the transition (　　　　　) a predominantly renewable-based future.
   再生できることを主軸に据えた未来への移行を促進する手段としての天然ガスや原子力の役割がある。

2. EU countries disagree (　　　　　) which fuels are truly sustainable.
   どの燃料が本当に持続可能なのかについて、EU 諸国の意見は一致していない。

3. In Japan, coal and natural gas need to be replaced (　　　　　) ammonia and hydrogen to convert existing fossil fuel plants (　　　　　) zero-emission facilities.
   日本において、既存の化石燃料プラントをゼロエミッション（排出ゼロ）設備に転換するためには、石炭や天然ガスをアンモニアや水素に置き換えることが必要である。

with　　　towards　　　into　　　on　　　as

Background Knowledge

 CD 2-43

欧州委員会が環境に良い事業への投資と認定する基準の草案内容について、本文に述べられているものを 1 ～ 4 から選びましょう。

A draft of the European Commission's proposal, seen by Reuters, would label nuclear power plant investments as green if the project has a plan, funds and a site to safely dispose of radioactive waste. To be deemed green, new nuclear plants must receive construction permits before 2045.

Investments in natural gas power plants would also be deemed green if they produce emissions below 270g of CO_2 equivalent per kilowatt hour (kWh), replace a more polluting fossil fuel plant, receive a construction permit by Dec. 31, 2030, and plan to switch to low-carbon gases by the end of 2035.   *Reuters*

Notes investment「投資」 deem...「～だとみなす」 CO_2 equivalent per kilowatt hour「1 キロワット時あたりの二酸化炭素換算量（さまざまな種類や質量の温室効果ガスに関して、地球温暖化への影響の大きさを二酸化炭素量に換算して統一的に表す尺度）」

1. 原子力発電所建設にあたっては、放射性廃棄物を安全に処理するための施設を先に建設しておかねばならない。
2. 2045 年までに原子力発電所の建設が完了する計画でなければならない。
3. 天然ガス発電所は、1 キロワット時あたりの二酸化炭素換算量が 270g 未満でなければならない。
4. 天然ガス発電所は、2035 年末までに建設許可を受けなければならない。

Newspaper English

 現在の文脈中に過去の助動詞が使用されているときは、仮定法と考えられます。伝える内容が不確実な場合や、推量的に物事を述べる場合に使われます。

以下の英文中の下線部を日本語に訳しましょう。

Brussels has made moves to apply the system to some EU funding, meaning the rules <u>could decide</u> which projects are eligible for certain public finance.

EU 本部は、この制度を一部の EU の資金援助に適用する動きも見せている。つまり、これらの規則が、どのプロジェクトが一定の公的融資を受ける資格があるのかを _____ _____ ということである。

Note Brussels「ブリュッセル（ここでは EU 本部のこと）」

Reading

EU drafts plan to label gas and nuclear investments as green

label... 「〜を分類する」

The European Union has drawn up plans to label some natural gas and nuclear energy projects as "green" investments after a year-long battle between governments over which investments are truly climate-friendly.

draw up... 「〜を作成する」

5　The European Commission is expected to propose rules in January deciding whether gas and nuclear projects will be included in the EU "sustainable finance taxonomy."

propose... 「〜を提案する」

This is a list of economic activities and the environmental criteria they must meet to be labelled as 10　green investments.

criteria　criterion（基準、指標）の複数形

By restricting the "green" label to truly climate-friendly projects, the system aims to make those investments more attractive to private capital, and stop "greenwashing," where companies or investors overstate their eco-friendly 15　credentials.

restrict... 「〜を限定する」

private capital 「民間資本」
investor 「投資家」
overstate... 「〜を誇張する」
credentials 「認証、資格」

Brussels has also made moves to apply the system to some EU funding, meaning the rules could decide which projects are eligible for certain public finance.

"Taking account of scientific advice and current 20　technological progress as well as varying transition challenges across member states, the Commission considers there is a role for natural gas and nuclear power as a means to facilitate the transition towards a predominantly renewable-based future," the European 25　Commission said in a statement.

take account of... 「〜を考慮する」
varying 「異なる、さまざまな」
member state 「加盟国」

statement 「声明」

To help states with varying energy backgrounds to transition, "under certain conditions, solutions can make sense that do not look exactly 'green' at first glance," a Commission source told Reuters, adding that gas and 30　nuclear investments would face "strict conditions." EU countries disagree on which fuels are truly sustainable.

state 「国」
make sense 「意味を持つ」
at first glance 「一見して」
source 「消息筋」

The EU's advisers had recommended that gas plants not be labelled as green investments unless they met a lower 100g CO_2e/kWh emissions limit, based on the deep 35　emissions cuts scientists say are needed to avoid

recommend... 「〜を勧告する」

CO_2e = carbon dioxide equivalent

disastrous climate change.

Nuclear power produces very low CO_2 emissions, but the Commission sought expert advice this year on whether the fuel should be deemed green given the potential
40 environmental impact of radioactive waste disposal.

Austria opposes nuclear power, alongside countries including Germany and Luxembourg. EU states including the Czech Republic, Finland and France, which gets around 70% of its power from the fuel, see nuclear energy
45 as crucial to phasing out CO_2-emitting coal fueled power.

Reuters

disastrous「悲惨な」

sought... seek（〜を求める）
の過去形
given...「〜を考えると」
potential「可能性のある」
oppose...「〜に反対する」

crucial「重要な」
phase out...「〜を段階的に廃
止する」

参考

· sustainable finance taxonomy (l. 7)「サステナブルファイナンス・タクソノミ」：
2020 年に EU が主導して公表された「持続可能性に貢献する経済活動」を分類する
基準のこと。今後も定期的に見直し・更新が行われる予定。
·greenwashing (l. 13)「グリーンウオッシュ」：企業などが消費者らへの訴求効果を狙っ
て環境に配慮しているかのように装うこと。

Comprehension

本文の内容に合うように、1 と 3 の質問の答えとして適当なものを、2 の英文を完成
させるのに適当なものを、a 〜 d から選びましょう。

1. Which of the following is NOT a stated purpose of the EU proposal?
   a. To decrease the amount of CO_2 emissions produced by nuclear power plants
   b. To stop exaggerated claims of environmentally-friendly practices by some companies
   c. To help member states with varying backgrounds transition to primarily renewable energy
   d. To increase investment in projects that do not cause harm to the environment

2. The European Commission specifically requested professional guidance about
   a. the environmental impact of radioactive waste disposal.
   b. a limit on the CO_2 emissions of gas power plants.
   c. the amount of radioactive waste that is safely disposable.
   d. an examination of the harmful 'greenwashing' effect.

3. Which country does not approve of the use of nuclear power?

   a. Finland

   b. Germany

   c. The Czech Republic

   d. France

Summary

 DL 57　　CD 2-45

以下の空所 1 〜 4 に当てはまる語を選択肢から選び、書き入れましょう。

> After much debate and a thorough examination of the latest scientific evidence, the European Union has produced a plan to ($^{1.}$　　　　　) nuclear power and natural gas projects as "green" investments. Though both energy sources have the potential to ($^{2.}$　　　　　) great harm to the environment, the proposal includes strict limits that must be met in order to ($^{3.}$　　　　　) the designation. The goal is to ($^{4.}$　　　　　) investment in environmentally friendly projects and move away from utilizing fossil fuels.

cause　　receive　　encourage　　label

Insights into Today's World

 DL 58　　CD 2-46

以下の対話の空所に、あなたの考えを書いてみましょう。その後、クラスメイトにその内容を伝えてみましょう。

Despite controversy over whether nuclear power and natural gas should be considered sustainable options, the EU plans to consider them "green" for investment purposes.
What do you think of the EU's policy?

I agree/disagree with it because _____

_____

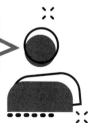

Chapter 20

Making Sense of the Metaverse

メタバースの時代、目の前の誰かが本物じゃなかったら？

Key Expressions 1

🎧 DL 59　◎ CD 2-47

音声を聞いて 1 ～ 3 の（　　）内に適当な語を書き入れましょう。

1. People experience eerie or (u _ _ _ _ _) feelings in response to humanoid robots that closely, but not perfectly, resemble human beings.

   人は、人間によく似てはいるが、完全には似ていないヒューマノイドロボットに対して、得体の知れない、もしくは不安な感情を覚える。

2. We are not sure about what happens as robots' (r _ _ _ _ _ _ _ _ _ _) to humans is perfected.

   我々は、ロボットの人間との類似性が完全になるにつれて何が起こるのか分かっていない。

3. Some researchers worry that as "trusted" virtual humans become indistinguishable from real people, we open ourselves to more (m _ _ _ _ _ _ _ _ _ _ _) by platform providers.

   研究者の中には、「信頼できる」仮想の人間が、実物の人間と区別がつかなくなるにつれて、我々はプラットフォームの提供者により操作されやすくなるのではと心配する者もいる。

Key Expressions 2

1 〜 5 は本文に出てくるデジタル分野の語句です。日本語訳を参考に、（　　）内に当てはまる語を選択肢から選び、書き入れましょう。

1. (　　　　　　　　　) fields 　　　　　急成長の分野
2. low-(　　　　　　　　　) 　　　　　低忠実度の
3. internet's next (　　　　　　　　　) 　インターネットの次のバージョン
4. (　　　　　　　　　) environment 　没入環境
5. (　　　　　　　　　) artificial agent 　義務優先型の人工エージェント

> immersive　　fidelity　　agenda-driven　　burgeoning　　iteration

参考
・没入環境：コンピュータが創り出すヴァーチャルな世界に入り込むこと。
・義務優先型：他人の意向に配慮するのでなく、義務・職務を優先すること。

Key Expressions 3

日本語訳を参考に、1 〜 3 の英文の（　　　　）内に当てはまる動詞を選択肢から選び、適当な時制にして書き入れましょう。

1. In 2021, Meta (　　　　　　　　　　　　) it would spend at least $10 billion on its metaverse division to create AR and VR hardware, software, and content.
   2021 年に、メタ社は AR や VR のハードウェア、ソフトウェア、そしてコンテンツを作るため、メタバース部門に少なくとも 100 億ドルを費やすと発表した。

2. Other tech companies, including Microsoft and video-game and software developer Epic Games, (　　　　　　　　　　　　) on the bandwagon since then.
   マイクロソフト社やビデオゲームとソフトウェアのデベロッパーであるエピック・ゲームズ社のような他のテック企業はそれ以来その流行に便乗してきた。

3. Nike Inc. (　　　　　　　　　　　　) Nikeland, featuring virtual sneakers, on video-game platform Roblox.
   ナイキ社は、ビデオゲームのプラットフォームのロブロックスに、ヴァーチャル・スニーカーを目玉とするナイキランドを立ち上げたところだ。

> launch　　jump　　announce

Background Knowledge

CD 2-48

ロボット工学の第一人者である森政弘東京工業大学名誉教授が提唱した説について、英文に<u>述べられていないもの</u>を1～4から選びましょう。

Mori, now 94, originally plotted his "uncanny valley" hypothesis in a graph, showing an observer's emotional response towards the human likeness of a robot.

He stated that as a robot's appearance is made more humanlike, there is a growing affinity for it but only up to a point beyond which the person experiences a reaction of extreme disgust, coldness, or even fear, shown by a plunge into the valley. But as the robot becomes more indistinguishable from a real person, positive emotions of empathy similar to human-to-human interaction emerge once more. The disconcerting void between "not-quite-human" and "perfectly human" is the uncanny valley.

Kyodo News

Notes　hypothesis「仮説」　affinity「好感度」　disgust「嫌悪」　plunge「落ち込み」　empathy「共感」

1. 彼は人間に似たロボットを「不気味の谷」と命名した。

2. 彼の説では、ロボットが人間に似るにつれて好感度が増すが、ある地点を超えるとかなりの嫌悪感を覚えるという。

3. 人はロボットが実物の人間と区別がつかないほど似てくると、再び好感を抱く。

4.「人間とは言えない」と「人間と全く同じ」との間にある隙が「不気味の谷」である。

Newspaper English

英文記事には様々な略語や頭字語が出てきます。基本的なものは覚えておきましょう。

日本語訳を参考に、以下の1～5の（　　　）内に適当な語を書き入れ、略語の正式名称を完成させましょう。

1. VR = (　　　　　　　　) Reality　　　　　　　　　　　　　仮想現実

2. CEO = (　　　　　　) (　　　　　　　　　　) Officer　代表取締役

3. 3D = 3 (　　　　　　　　)　　　　　　　　　　　　　　　三次元の

4. AR = (　　　　　　　　) Reality　　　　　　　　　　　　　拡張現実

5. AI = (　　　　　　　　) (　　　　　　　　　　　)　　　人工知能

Reading

Is the 'uncanny valley' good for a future metaverse?

TOKYO — It has been over five decades since Japanese roboticist Masahiro Mori developed a theory describing the eerie or uneasy feeling people experience in response to humanoid robots that closely, but not perfectly, resemble human beings.

describe... 「〜を説明する」

Labeled the "uncanny valley" by Mori in 1970, the phenomenon has stood the test of time with more recent examples of creepiness filtering into the burgeoning fields of artificial intelligence, photorealistic computer animation, virtual reality, augmented reality, and increasingly lifelike androids.

stand the test of the time 「時の検証に耐える」
creepiness 「不気味さ」
filter into... 「〜に入り込む」

But what happens beyond the other side of the valley as resemblance to humans is perfected? Some researchers worry that as "trusted" virtual humans become indistinguishable from real people, we open ourselves to more manipulation by platform providers. In other words, our responses while still in the uncanny valley, as creepy as they can be, could be a good thing — a kind of self-defense mechanism.

self-defense mechanism 「自己防衛機制」

With tech companies led by Mark Zuckerberg's Meta Platforms Inc. staking a claim on the creation of a metaverse — viewed as the internet's next iteration "where people can work and socialize in a virtual world" — some experts say the uncanny valley graph is just as pertinent in immersive environments, including in VR and AR.

stake a claim on... 「〜に対する権利を主張する」
socialize 「交流する」
pertinent 「しっくりくる、妥当な」

While we have become accustomed to interacting with "low-fidelity versions of human faces going back to the early days of TV," we will have the ability to project photorealistic humans in 3D virtual worlds before the end of this decade, Louis Rosenberg, a 30-year veteran of AR development and CEO of Unanimous AI, recently told Kyodo News in an interview. How will we determine what is real?

"Personally, I believe the greatest danger of the metaverse is the prospect that agenda-driven artificial

prospect 「予想」

agents controlled by AI algorithms will engage us in 'conversational manipulation' without us realizing that the 'person' we are interacting with is not real."

40 In a corporate-controlled metaverse featuring "virtual product placement," we could easily think we are simply having a conversation with a person like ourselves, causing us to drop our defenses. "You won't know what was manipulated to serve the agenda of a paying third-party and what is authentic."

45 This is dangerous because "the AI agent that is trying to influence us could have access to a vast database about our personal interests and beliefs, purchasing habits, temperament, etc. So how do we protect against this? Regulation," Rosenberg said.

Kyodo News

engage... 「～を巻き込む」	
placement 「配置」	
paying third-party 「儲けている第三者」	
authentic 「本物の」	
beliefs 「信念」	
temperament 「気質」	

● **Comprehension**

本文の内容に合うように、1と2の英文を完成させるのに適当なものを、3の質問の答えとして適当なものを、a～dから選びましょう。

1. Masahiro Mori's "uncanny valley" theory describes

   a. humanity's hesitation to adopt the latest technologies.

   b. the unpleasant response people have to certain humanoid robots.

   c. a person's inability to trust androids that perfectly resemble humans.

   d. the trend toward robots becoming increasingly humanlike.

2. Louis Rosenberg believes the most concerning aspect of a corporate-controlled metaverse is that

   a. there are not enough laws to regulate tech companies.

   b. people will be expected to purchase many virtual products.

   c. artificial agents may be employed to exploit users.

   d. third parties may have inaccurate information about customers.

3. According to Rosenberg, what is the solution to the problems he describes?

   a. Educating metaverse users on the dangers of artificial agents

   b. Removing corporate control of the metaverse

   c. A set of rules protecting metaverse users

   d. An increase in authentic human interactions

Summary

🎧 DL 60　◎ CD 2-50

以下の空所 1 ～ 4 に当てはまる語を選択肢から選び、書き入れましょう。

> 　Rapid advancements in technology are ($^{1.}$　　　　　　　　　　)
> to the possibility that people will soon find themselves working and
> socializing in virtual environments and ($^{2.}$　　　　　　　　　)
> with artificial agents projected as photorealistic humans. In such a case,
> people may have trouble ($^{3.}$　　　　　　　　　) between real
> humans and artificial agents. Given the corporate control of such agents,
> along with possible access to users' private information, experts are
> ($^{4.}$　　　　　　　　) of the potential for manipulation.

warning　　distinguishing　　interacting　　leading

Insights into Today's World

🎧 DL 61　◎ CD 2-51

以下の対話の空所に、あなたのアイデアを書いてみましょう。その後、クラスメイト
にその内容を伝えてみましょう。

It seems that the virtual world is really becoming part of our lives. I saw a humanoid robot on TV the other day. I felt a little creepy because it didn't really move quite like a human.
Do you think you would feel the same if you encountered a robot like that?

I am not sure, but _____

_____

Acknowledgements

All the news materials are reprinted by permission of

The Japan News, The Asahi Shimbun Asia & Japan Watch, The Mainichi, Kyodo News,
The Associated Press, AFP-JIJI Press and Reuters.

TEXT CREDITS

Chapter 1   Being Eco-Friendly with Edible Tableware

Reduce waste with edible tableware

The Japan News, May 4, 2021 (partially modified)

Chapter 2   In Search of More Fluid Styles of Work

Employees exploring new work options amid coronavirus pandemic

The Japan News, September 17, 2021 (partially modified)

Chapter 3   Cats Don't Look, but They Know

Study: Cats know masters' location through hearing, not sight

The Asahi Shimbun Asia & Japan Watch, December 29, 2021 (partially modified)

Chapter 4   Challenges of a High School Entrepreneur

15-yr-old in Japan turns hardship with hypersensitivity into fashion, support business

The Mainichi, October 7, 2021 (partially modified)

Chapter 5   The Ties that Bind Hearts

"Mizuhiki" Japanese knot-tying giving connection to cultural heritage

Kyodo News, December 26, 2021 (partially modified)

Chapter 6   Insect Funerals

Funeral services to honor pet insects gain quiet popularity in Japan

The Mainichi, December 31, 2021 (partially modified)

Chapter 7   The History of QR Codes

From Japanese auto parts to ubiquity: a look at the history of QR codes

The Mainichi, November 10, 2021 (partially modified)

Chapter 8   Afghanistan's Bacha Posh

Afghan girls get to be boys, for limited time

The Associated Press, December 8, 2021 (partially modified)

Chapter 9   Buy a Drink, Change the World

'Donation vending machines' help buyers give back

The Japan News, November 17, 2021 (partially modified)

Chapter 10   Real × Unreal

Anime x Paris Fashion Week / Anrealage's online collection opens up whole new world

The Japan News, January 20, 2022 (partially modified)

本書には音声CD（別売）があります

Insights 2023
世界を読むメディア英語入門2023

2023年 1 月20日 初版第 1 刷発行
2023年 2 月20日 初版第 2 刷発行

編著者　　村　尾　純　子
　　　　　深　山　晶　子
　　　　　辻　本　智　子
　　　　　横　山　香　奈
　　　　　Christopher Cladis

発行者　　福　岡　正　人
発行所　　株式会社　金　星　堂
〒101-0051 東京都千代田区神田神保町3-21
Tel. (03) 3263-3828（営業部）
(03) 3263-3997（編集部）
Fax (03) 3263-0716
https://www.kinsei-do.co.jp

編集担当　蔦原美智　　　　　　　　Printed in Japan
印刷所・製本所／萩原印刷株式会社

ISBN978-4-7647-4173-7　C1082